THE
JOY
WEAVER
grassroots

Nancy McComb
Nancy McComb

Copyright © 2022 by Nancy McComb
Cover Illustration © 2022 by Sheri Roberts
Cover Design © 2023 by Brady McComb and Ben Merillat
All Rights Reserved
Printed in the United States of America
ISBN: 979-8-9875603-0-3

Scripture quotations are taken from the New American Standard Bible®, Copyright © The Lockman Foundation 1995, as published on biblegateway.com. Used by permission of The Zondervan Corporation. All rights reserved.

Names of some individuals in this book are changed.

All font of this type shows journal excerpts.

No part of this publication may be reproduced or stored in any format without written permission from the author publisher, except for brief quotations embodied in printed reviews.

Requests for written permission may be directed to:

Mrs. Nancy McComb
TheJoyWeaverCommunity@gmail.com
Lexington, South Carolina, USA

DEDICATION

Mom and Dad,
faithful and obedient disciples of Christ
who modeled how to walk with a Holy God
as imperfect people.
I am eternally grateful to God for giving me you both.
I love you! You are good to me!

TABLE OF CONTENTS

Preface with Acknowledgments	9
Introduction	15
Epigraph	16
1 HONDURAN HACIENDA SNAPSHOTS	17
2 YOU SHALL NOT LIE	27
3 YOU SHALL NOT STEAL	30
4 MORNING GLORY	33
5 *Golden Rag Memories*	37
6 MISSION TRANSITION	40
7 A FIRM FOUNDATION	45
8 ALOHA	53
9 THE 30-DAY CHALLENGE	57
10 A NEW CREATION	61
11 UNASHAMED	65
12 AWANA	69
13 A WHALE OF A TALE	72
14 BEAUTIFUL MUSIC	78
15 A WISE MOVE	83
16 ON EAGLE'S WINGS	87
17 DEDICATED	92

18 *Praise and Dedication*   94

19 BE ANXIOUS FOR NOTHING   95

20 DISTRACTED   100

21 *In His Time*   106

22 A FIRM FOUNDATION FOR DATING   109

23 DOUBLE-MINDED   114

24 *Heartache*   119

25 YOU COULDN'T PAY ME   120

26 MY EARNEST PLEA   124

27 BIG HOUSE – LOTS OF KIDS   129

28 *Transition*   132

29 THE NUT HOUSE   134

30 HIS HANDIWORK I SEE   139

31 THE LONELY YEAR   144

32 *New Song*   154

33 BIG BEAR BURDEN   156

34 THE POWER OF PRAYER AND PRAISE   161

35 A BOY NAMED BILL MCCOMB   167

36 BEST FRIEND TO THE RESCUE   171

37 PENITENCE AND IMPATIENCE   177

38 CHENANIAH CHEER   181

39 HOW DEEP IS YOUR LOVE	189
40 IT'S OFFICIAL	195
41 AND SO IT BEGINS	199
Glossary	214
End Notes	215

PREFACE WITH ACKNOWLEDGMENTS

A pen in my hand is as tantalizing as a Lindt chocolate truffle in my mouth. Tapping fingers on a keyboard is only slightly less appealing. Stories, journals, poems, emails, snail mail, sermon notes, school notes, research reports, essays, legal documents, or "to do" lists - the bottom line is that I love to write!

Perhaps being an author was on my bucket list back in kindergarten. I was a Third Culture Kid (TCK) at Academia Los Pinares in Honduras, Central America. The horse tale my class and I created is tucked here in my filing cabinet to this day. Colorful waxy crayon illustrations join the whimsical story displayed on sheets of soft cream-colored newsprint. Childish handwriting is generally wedged between those highway-like lines, broken down the middle and solid on either side.

In third grade, having moved to Hawaii, a friend from church loaned me Nancy Drew and Hardy Boy mysteries. The whodunnit genre inspired me to write and self-publish *The Case of the Missing Hamburgers*. The long formica desk Dad and Mom acquired at a hotel renovation sale afforded me a spacious place to work my craft. Despite tremendous dedication, I was a novice in story formulation. Of course the McDonald's Hamburglar stole the irresistible meat patties tucked into soft white buns. The only real thing missing in my marvelous mystery was a plot twist!

In fourth grade at Aikahi Elementary, we crushed rectangles of brown paper bag into "snowballs," then flattened them out by rubbing our hands across the wrinkles. I remember tickling my palms across the soft, uneven ridges. Paint brushes, potato stamps and brown paint helped us decorate the tapa cloth facsimiles with

Nancy McComb

flowers, stripes, and geometric shapes. These works of art became book covers for research on the Hawaiian Islands. Embarrassingly, this assignment displayed my prolific spelling problems. Red circles were slung around words all over my rough draft!

The next year I studied word endings: -ent or -ant, -ence or -ance, -cious or -tious. Memorizing homophones gave me the rites to write the right words. I doubled down on words like apple butter fritters and anchored a subtle knack for wrestling ghost characters. We practiced where apostrophes belonged and diagrammed complex sentences. At the provocation of a competitive classmate, I glamorized my cursive. This turned out to be profitable because my parents rewarded me $1 for every top grade on my report card. I was thriving in these linguistic pursuits.

Our zany but lovable fifth grade teacher required the same class project every year. Each student created a scrapbook of newspaper headlines and articles. We had to label our pages "Who?" "What?" "Where?" "When?" "Why?" and "How? Cutting and pasting littered the floor with discarded scraps from the excerpts of stories we affixed under each title. Elmer's glue ran amuck on papers, hands, and desktops. If too many of us approached the teacher for help, she got nervous. She would rub her palms together, rotating a pinched pencil topped with twisted red troll hair. Spinning the yellow No. 2 wildly back and forth would fray the red mop, as if it had burst into flames. "Get away from my desk!" she would warn frantically. But she taught us well.

Building homemade books equaled the satisfaction of developing their content. Rectangles cut from boxes or backs of memo pads provided the spine and boards. Wallpaper or cloth samples would be secured to the whole outside, with protruding flaps folded inside and glued down. Glued-down flaps inside the boards were then covered over with end paper left to right, crossing the middle to produce smooth and tidy hinges. This whole

THE JOY WEAVER - GRASSROOTS

binding, folded along its joints, became the cover.

A stack of papers, sewn or stapled as a book block, would be glued inside the spine. Rather than making a dust jacket, I would affix a narrow rectangle of coordinating colored paper to the outside edge of the book on which to write the title. A matching-colored paper square up front would also display title and author.

In eighth grade at St. Mark's Lutheran School, I had procrastinated again! Mom offered to transform my dictated rough draft into the final copy of a report on Amadeus Wolfgang Mozart. She was and is a fabulous administrative assistant and proficient typist. The electric typewriter in her church office and her efficient clerical speed would make the drive worth it for both of us.

The workstation in the narrow portable filled with a symphony of success. Keys clicked and clacked like castanets in the percussion section. The carriage return chimed at the end of each measure. And the cylinder zipped in crescendo as each sheet rolled out. Noting the last page, I stapled the black and white masterpiece together and tucked it into a sturdy orange manila folder. The front was decorated with a xeroxed picture of the wild-haired composer. This was my longest research project to date!

Writing during my freshman year of high school at the Hawaii Baptist Academy proved to be a difficult battle. Term papers and book reports returned like wounded soldiers, marred with the crimson stains of my English teacher's red pen. Mrs. Rediger had memorized the MLA Handbook! With an impeccable grasp of grammar statutes, she authoritatively coded every infraction and meticulously screened every revision. I felt defeated at first, but soon grew to appreciate her as a hero among educators. She was a commander who inspired a high level of excellence.

Mr. Wally's animated instructions in tenth grade Creative Writing inspired artful expression. Dynamic word combinations in black and white could project colorful objects and ideas onto the cognitive canvas of the connoisseur. All semester we improvised verbal showpieces that would reincarnate evocative scenes, sensations, and experiences in a reader's imagination. I learned to exchange dreamy and dramatic overlays with poignant models and mosaics. "The most horrific pain ever" became "my heart crushed by barbed wire." "The most beautiful sunrise ever" became "the grape and tangerine glow of morning sun upon cotton candy clouds."

Another tenth-grade writing assignment, on the subject of twins, deeply piqued my interest. Double trouble? Or two-for-one special? I held fascination with the idea of winning that biological lottery. Genetic research seemed to count me out, so I had no real hope of being that blessed. Obviously, I didn't know much about the prophetic nature of God in those days. That introduction to reproductive science was the foreshadowing of a special inheritance in my marriage and family!

In preparing to graduate high school before attending college, I entered a writing scholarship contest. My story was packed with warmth, sorrow, and Christian virtue. Warmth was a close family, gathered for Christmas festivities by the flame-filled stone hearth. Sorrow was the orphan shivering outside in a ditch full of snow. Christian virtue was the family inviting her inside, having seen her through the full frosted living room window. Two weeks later, the reviewer handed it back to me unrewarded. The sense of being ordinary washed over me like drenching rain. A valuable lesson on the meaning of cliché had cost me more humiliation than time.

At Southwestern Bible College (SWC) in Phoenix, AZ, I faced my greatest writing challenges yet. As we discussed Calvinism and Armenianism in theology class, the purported Biblical contradictions were inescapably disturbing. Finding my professor in the cafeteria at lunch one day, I went down on my knees weeping. I had to know how influential giants, John Calvin and Jacob

THE JOY WEAVER - GRASSROOTS

Arminius, could instigate such tragic division in the Body of Christ. They were both Christians. They were both reading the Bible. If these two godly intellects could not reach agreement, how could I discern the truth? I toiled arduously over a contemplative research paper, seeking to correlate the doctrines of predestination and free will.

Over Christmas break, my dad listened to what I had learned in my research. And he in turn shared from his years of pondering these difficult truths. He had gone to Bible college, completed a master's degree in Biblical Studies and was a Professor at the International Baptist Bible College in Honolulu, Hawaii. I had high regard for him as a devoted follower of Christ. Holy Spirit gave me a firm conviction that God's teachings could not possibly contradict one another. There had to be a harmonious explanation made possible by considering all Scriptures collaboratively.

The 600-page volume of systematic theology in another class disheartened me as well. It also seemed to foster confusion and skepticism about Holy Scripture rather than a unified understanding of it. For example, was the rapture going to come before, during or after the tribulation? We were divided into three groups and assigned a debate.

Every position cited many Bible verses. Were we to determine that some passages were right, and some were wrong? The conflicting interpretations on this topic and many more were creating wedges among believers instead of binding us together on inerrant Truth. These divisions opposed God's desire that we "come together in one accord." Our disunity was confusing to unbelievers. I was annoyed.

I walked out of class one day saying, "I'm going to write a book called *Rubber Meets the Road Theology*." It would showcase testimonies from all types of Christians who had witnessed and applied Biblical truths in daily life. I wanted to show that the Bible is not only inerrant and authoritative, but essential and practical.

Nancy McComb

As a missionary kid (MK), having attended Mennonite, public, Lutheran, Southern Baptist and Conservative Baptist schools, I longed for all Christians to love, respect, and hunger for God's Word in unified celebration: as one body, baptized in one Spirit, serving one Lord, on one indivisible foundation, God's true Word.

    I knew my goal was possible "someday." But when? Growing up was all I seemed able to manage. I was busy! Five decades in, I've finally slowed down. "Someday" is TODAY. Many more books are now rolling around in my brain. Here we go!

INTRODUCTION

In the summer of 2018, as our youngest sons were heading to college, God spontaneously gifted me with a writing coach and a book title at church one morning. Deb and *The Joy Weaver* resonated with my heart and mind four-fold. First, I had approached Deb about a women's prayer group and found myself paired to an avid word smith with years of experience. Second, I had been gearing up to write books for our sons detailing God's teachings, interventions, and miracles over the years. Third, because Joy Weaver is my cousin, whom you will meet briefly in this book. And fourth, the Weaver bird is indigenous to Senegal, West Africa, where our family served at Dakar Academy for many years. Clearly, it was time to get started!

Testimonies of God's presence, protection and provision stretch beyond a hundred in the McComb home! Detailing His visible works will fill more than one book. Since God began transforming this willful girl from childhood, I bounced back to the beginning. *The Joy Weaver: grassroots* is a collection of whimsical and poignant tales of a mischievous, boy-crazy missionary kid (MK) growing up in Honduras and Hawaii. As often as I pledged my allegiance, I struggled to be faithful. But God - Father, Son, and Holy Spirit - is faithful. Despite obstacles we face or create, God is The Joy Weaver intertwining our lives with grace, wisdom, and joy as we learn to walk with Him. Surrender to His love with me and never look back.

Romans 8:28 *"And we know that God causes all things to work together for good to those who love God, to those who are called according to His purpose."*

"O Lord, You are my God;
I will exalt you,
I will give thanks to Your name;
For You have worked wonders,
Plans formed long ago,
with perfect faithfulness."

Isaiah 25:1

"Come and hear, all who fear God.
And I will tell of what He has done for my soul."

Psalm 66:16

"Let everything that has breath praise the Lord.
Praise the Lord!"

Psalm 150:6

1 HONDURAN HACIENDA SNAPSHOTS

The first place I called home was a 3-bedroom 2-bath rental house in Tegucigalpa, Honduras. It was constructed of grey cement blocks and cement tile floors. Air and light danced into the house through wide louvered windows. The landlord had let Dad build an addition on back where the bedroom hallway used to end. The big new family room was a fun hangout! I could grab a book and nestle into a stretchy rope chair of blue and black strings woven around black rebar frames. Other times, my brother John, Mom, Dad, and I would huddle up to play Yahtzee, Clue, or Boggle.

My parents would invite friends to rack and break balls on Dad's homemade pool table or round up in a circle for games. A worldwide missionary favorite was "The Dictionary Game." Someone would spell a weird word from Webster's Dictionary for everyone to write down. The rest of us would come up with our own definitions and then take turns reading them aloud. We counted votes for believable ones or popular funny fakes. One time, I was laughing so hard at my idea that no one could understand what I was trying to read aloud; and I nearly peed my pants!

Around the family table, Dad, Mom, John, and I would hold hands and give thanks to Heavenly Father before every meal. If it was first thing in the morning, my brother and I might be distracted by the box of Kaboom cereal sitting there unopened. Somewhere among those wheat bites and clown marshmallows was a buried treasure in the box. It might be a snap-together train sealed in cellophane, a plastic ring, or a race car. But only one of us would get to keep the collectible prize!

Many mornings after breakfast, Mom or Dad would read The Chronicles of Narnia, or the Bible, or a devotional book. I will never forget the story from *Devotions for the Children's Hour* by Kenneth N. Taylor (Moody Press, Chicago ©1954). God saw and disciplined a man who was going to steal watermelons from a field that was not his. His troubles impressed upon me that God is always watching us, and our sins will find us out!

John and I took turns setting dishes out for supper each night. It seemed such a chore, though Mom had spent hours preparing economical recipes from scratch. She was a good cook! Stuffed peppers were lamented, and cow tongue banished forever. But most of the time, her thrifty meals were delicious and nutritious. We still replicate family favorites like Ham Casserole: crunchy bread cubes and grated cheese, on top of scrumptious layers of ham, peas, and more bread cubes with cheese, swathed in bubbling white sauce. Yum!

And Mom loved to have fun! She relished surprises like a Black Cow (Coke in milk) or a creative alternative to the usual, like open-faced grilled cheese toast with grape jelly. While we ate, we talked. During meals, our family would indulge in sweet, savory, or saucy conversations: sharing thoughts, telling stories, or attending to necessities of the day.

The wood stereo cabinet Dad built for the living room housed a cassette player and a record player. A stack of record albums in sturdy cardboard jackets leaned behind a cupboard door. The bent arm with the glass-tipped needle at the end would tickle the rotating grooves on black plastic discs to emit tunes by Sesame

THE JOY WEAVER - GRASSROOTS

Street, The Gaithers, Ray Conniff, Jr., and B.J. Thomas. I would sway in the soundwaves bouncing around the room like water in a swimming pool. And I felt *On Top of The World* when I sang boisterously with Karen Carpenter's 45RPM hit single! My soul would swoon, sob, or soar with the intensity of each composition.

I watched with admiration the time Dad created a groovy lamp to hang from the ceiling, in the corner by the couch. He cut around the circumference of a brown glass gallon jug, removing the top, neck and finger hold with a glass cutter. Then he installed a light socket and bulb in the other end, attached to a wire passing through a tiny central hole in the inverted jug. The long wire was woven back and forth through a chain all the way to the plug. The inside wall of the amber-colored glass shell was lined with lightweight wire mesh. Finally, the lamp was hung, dangling from a hook in the ceiling, and plugged in. Muted light sprayed sideways in geometric shapes on the walls. Bright white light fell below for reading on the couch.

In the carport, Dad once pretended to stab himself with an extended radio antenna unscrewed from the hood of the car. The silly drama entertained me and my brother. We caught on quickly that the sections of antenna collapsed into one another as Dad pushed it against his stomach and humorously feigned tragedy.

In the tiny side yard behind the carport was the swing set Dad had built. It faced the back door and window of the kitchen. Mom could keep an eye on us from inside. I loved to swing endlessly, belting out songs as I oscillated. One day I sang *Raindrops Keep Falling on My Head*, repetitively mixing up the lyrics. Mom called out, chuckling from her workstation, "If you're not going to sing it right, don't sing it at all!"

It was also funny, though painful, the day I literally flew by the window in a green sweater, having slipped off the smooth seat at a high point! I'm sure it hurt, but Mom's attentive concern always motivated me to get up and brush off!

On the opposite side of the house, butted up to the outside wall of my parents' bedroom, was a huge rectangular trough, lined with cement and bordered by bricks. The garden hose gushing in there for an hour or two would create a shallow pool for us to splash around in. Or, if it was empty and dry, we could corral a litter of puppies from wandering off before their eyes had opened. It was fun to cuddle and romp with those adorable helpless creatures, as long as we avoided all their poop!

Several dogs kept us company over the years: Zipper the mutt mama, Buccaneer the German Shepherd, a descendant of the TV star Rin Tin Tin, Ginger the Dachshund, and Muffin. She was a puppy we had kept from one of our litters, who did not respond to my greeting one morning. As I searched the yard all over, I determined she was missing. Mom showed me the spot under the fence where someone could have coaxed her out night before. Had she been stolen? The unpreventable loss of someone I loved was gut-wrenching. I felt powerless!

Yet flying in my dreams was a different story! I would run with my arms spread out and fall forward onto the breeze. My body would gently lift into the air to glide wherever I pleased. It was a thrill to soar at great heights, observing the landscape below, then maneuvering a precarious landing with an adrenaline rush from thousands of feet up. It was refreshingly real to me.

So, when I was awake, I would go outside and perch on top of the open-brick wall in front of our entryway sidewalk. Taking slow deep breaths, I would imagine myself weightless. Then counting down, I would prepare myself to launch out over our front yard. "One, two, three," and *jump* on "four!" I so earnestly attempted to soar as effortlessly as I did in my dreams. Yet disappointingly, and without fail, my light-hearted body would plunge to the ground like a helium balloon tied to bricks.

I learned other down-to-earth lessons around the giant tree in our front yard. Losing my balance from up inside the lush canopy one day, I came bumping and thumping through branch after branch and finally smacked hard on the ground. Gravity was such an inescapable force, scarring me with skid-marks and bruises.

Resting under the tree another day, I begged Heavenly Father in Jesus' name for a baby black bear. Each time, I closed my eyes tight while praying, and then popped them open with big faith to receive my adorable prize. Though I earnestly invoked the promise of **John 15:16b** *"...whatever you ask of the Father in My name He may give to you,"* I finally had to concede it must not be God's will.

Another day in my room, however, I experienced a significant answer to prayer that assured me God was listening. One Christmas, Dad had built me a play-sized kitchen cupboard with a sink. Mom had saved all varieties of food storage containers to use while I pretended to cook. Alas, I had lost my butter box! Though I looked high and low, I could not find it anywhere.

I prayed, "Dear Heavenly Father, please help me find my butter box. You know right where it is." As soon as I opened my eyes, I was drawn to look across my room. And there it was, tucked underneath a book that was lodged across the V-shaped seat section of my rope chair! In that startling moment, I was keenly aware that the Holy Spirit had guided me!

I was not very tidy as a youngster. I had gleefully followed Mom around the house when I was tiny, and someday I would strive to emulate her cleanliness, especially in bathrooms and kitchens. But during my primary school years and beyond, taking care of my room was a drudge. Why make the bed in the morning just to pull back the covers at night? Why throw away trash that might become a treasure? Why organize clothes if I didn't care much about what I was wearing?

My mom's parents, Grandma and Grandpa, came to visit us in Honduras. Grandpa had volunteered to encourage me in spring cleaning. At first alone in my bedroom, miffed about the obligatory assignment, I used my forearm to bulldoze aggravating piles of cubby contents onto the floor. I yanked miscellaneous objects from under the bed. A jumbled mess from the tile floor of my closet was thrust into the open. I herded it all into a heap in the center of my room. The hill of toys and clothes and trash and dirty laundry was overwhelming, so I just sat on it…and ate my sugar.

Yup. One thing I had rescued from tumbling off a cubby shelf was a Styrofoam cup of white sugar. It was covered with a Kleenex and sealed securely around the lip with a rubber band. I loved eating plain sugar! If unobserved, I would bend my head back at the dining table, with Mom's yellow flip-lid Tupperware tipped over my gaping mouth. Sweet crystals tumbled like a waterfall on my salivating tongue.

This Kleenex-covered cup had been horded in my room as a secret stash. There I was munching on it when Grandpa came into my room to check my progress. He was shocked. "Oh, Nancy!" I still remember his exasperated yet affectionate huff. I thought the scene was hilarious, but I finally got serious and cleaned it up!

Sometimes we endured difficult events not of our choosing. One of our maids had been stealing clothes and kitchen items, so my parents had been obligated to fire her. Then, while we were away on home assignment, the couple subletting our house had hired her back, even though we had warned them not to. When we returned, she was gone again, as were more of our household possessions, and even some of our toys!

Another maid locked me in my room one night while my parents were out. I must have provoked her because after she led me there, she shut off the light and angrily closed and locked my door. I wailed with fearful tears in the pitch black, sliding along the wall, groping desperately for the light switch! I don't recall ever being rescued or comforted. Perhaps I finally lay still on my bed and escaped into sleep.

Darkness taunted my childhood imaginations. After nightly prayers and kisses with Mom and Dad, my blackened room would feel thick and alive. I knew Jesus was with me, and I enjoyed my time pondering and praying with Him. But for many years, I could not let my feet hang over the bed. I imagined creepy monkeys underneath, waiting to grab a protruding limb. Closet doors were always closed to protect me from the beady red eyes and leering shadows. These ghostly fears and sensitivities to the supernatural followed me place to place, far into my adulthood.

I absolutely hated getting shots! I am certain I embarrassed my parents during the administration of a smallpox vaccine when I was a little girl in Honduras. Medical attendants had to hold onto my scaredy-girl arms from both sides as I shrieked and shirked the approaching needle. It was terrifying! I obtained immunity to smallpox and a round pock-marked scar on the side of my arm. But I bore a deeper scar in my sense of well-being. An ominous injection-wielding robot chased me in a nightmare that sent me scurrying to the foot of my parents' bed through pitch black fear.

Vivid scenes of MK life in that far-off land played in my mind like movie trailers as I grew up. Once I told my mom about remembering the flight in a Cessna with their friends, the Dennises. A tribal man deep in the Honduran bush had sliced his arm with a machete, so we had been making our way there to offer emergency care. I could still "look" out the plane window with my head on the glass, staring at the land below. I could still "walk" on the smooth dirt floor into the doorway of the stick hut where he was holding his arm. Mom responded, "You were only two!"

Behind the Dennises' missionary house, situated on a hill above a river, I watched local women make bars of soap with lye. When the lumps dried, they soaped and scrubbed their clothes on the rocks, using them like washboards. Then each garment was carefully laid out flat in the sun to dry. Handmade soaps still trigger those sentimental memories and a deep respect for hard work.

Missionary potlucks at Parque Aurora were as jolly as a circus! Leafy branches flapped in the breeze like showbiz flags. Sunshine spotlighted the bustling crew of friends setting the stage near pine tree towers under the big top of blue sky. Sir David loved to perform. He would snatch the red-and-white-checked tablecloth out from under a pillar of Coke bottles, hoping not to topple them. What a clown!

Following a picnic lunch, John, Abner, my buddy Esther and I, and others, marched on parade down the trail to enjoy "spinning saucer" tricks on the merry-go-round. As daylight dove headfirst into darkness, families would pile into their cars and scurry home. We might pause to eat hot *pupusas* at a food shack nestled near the winding mountain road. Mesmerized by the day's entertainment, we'd finally hit the hay back home.

Dad had two motorcycles; one of them he built himself. I was ecstatic the day he put me on the back seat and plopped a helmet on my head, ready to venture down our driveway and out the front gate. I held onto him tight as we mingled with the hustle and bustle of taxis, sedans, bicycles, buses, men with *sombreros*, women with *bolsas*, *burros* and *pollos*, and food carts of *pinas*, *mansanas*, *mangos* and *café*.

I ingested the audiovisual chaos, smells of diesel fumes and road sweat, and braved the bumpety-bump of uneven pavement and occasional potholes. Beautiful brown people adorned the Honduran city sidewalks donning red clothes, yellow clothes, blue clothes, white clothes, and multi-colored clothes. Dad and I tried to talk, but the whipping wind whisked our words away. Trip done, we circled back to the carport and dismounted. I had a lot to tell Mom!

Then came a grown-up adventure without my parents in second grade! I had earned a spot to represent Los Pinares in a local spelling bee. It was exhilarating to leave home on an overnighter in another town at 8 years old! Mom gave me a pint-sized milk carton filled with foiled chocolates for the road. I was savoring them in my seat before we ever left! I felt fancy in my new red corduroy pants and beautiful beige Winnie-the-Pooh blouse with poofy sleeves. As our bus pulled into the hotel that evening, I became aware I had left my bathing suit behind. Everything within me groaned. No matter! Not skipping swimming, I slipped into the pool anyway. Heavy clothes were not going to drown my enthusiasm. This was high adventure!

When it came near time to perform the next morning, I felt jittery, unprepared, unsure, unable to reach ahead for the keys to conquer a challenge I could not see. What if I failed? I wanted to win so badly. When they finally called my name, and gave me the word I was to spell, I stood frozen while my brain raced between various possibilities. And then came time to commit to a response. I spelled the word wait, "W – A – T – E." Oh no. I heard the judges' sad sighs. How could I have fumbled so early in the contest with such a small word? I was so disappointed in myself! I was sure I should have lasted a lot longer.

Back home, there were oodles of love and encouragement to go around. Surely, my stories about that trip left us all shaking our heads and laughing. Unfortunately, through the years, there would also be arguments and deep discouragements in our family interactions. Such is life. God was big at our house, and we knew we were little. The nearness of His presence, the clarity of His Word, and the purity of His love would be the power to save, heal, and deliver us, one day and one year at a time.

1 Thessalonians 5:23-24 *"Now may the God of peace Himself sanctify you entirely; and may your spirit and soul and body be preserved complete, without blame at the coming of our Lord Jesus Christ. Faithful is He who calls you, and He also will bring it to pass."*

2 YOU SHALL NOT LIE

Honduras is in Central America. It borders Guatemala on the northwest, El Salvador on the southwest, and Nicaragua on the southeast. This small mountainous country varies in temperatures depending on elevation. Lowlands average 80°. Mountain basins and valleys average about 70°.[1] When I was six months old, my parents took me from Puerto Rico to live in Tegucigalpa, the capital city of Honduras. Centrally located on hilly terrain, Teguc (*Tay-goose*) ran anywhere from 50-90°. It could be uncomfortably warm and humid at times.[2] I spent eight years of my childhood there, until we moved away the summer after second grade.

Having now experienced the scorching heat of Arizona and West Africa for most of my adult life, I cannot imagine why ice chips were such an "irresistible" temptation to me as an MK in that far more pleasant climate. But I do remember craving them. Certainly, the cost of obtaining them could not have been worth the grief I caused my family!

Our square freezer compartment below the fridge was a haven of bulging ice, and I knew just the tool to dislodge the surplus buildup. The sharp-tipped metal ice pick could chip away fluffy chilly chunks with ease. I would pop one into my mouth and enjoy the crunchy cool refreshment between my teeth, joining in with the saliva on my tongue, and then trickling like a bubbling brook down my throat…unless it got stuck to my lips first!

At some point, Mom had discovered my unwise habit. She taught me about the danger of poking an ice pick into those miniature glaciers. The tubing beneath the metal wall of the freezer compartment carried a refrigerant called freon, which enabled the freezer to preserve foods at ice-cold temperatures. If the pointed tip of the ice pick ever punctured those tubes, the gas would escape and permanently ruin the freezer. You would think that ominous prospect would have held me at bay! But my stubborn will foolishly persisted in calculated secrecy.

One day, sneaky and happy, I was chipping away at my treat. And then the inevitable occurred. I had accidentally punched too hard, straight toward the metal lining! The sharp tip sank into the sidewall, like a toothpick into a cake. I tugged it out urgently and heard a slight hissing sound. OH NO! As I stood wondering what to do, wishing desperately this was not happening, praying that the sound would stop, my mind was already working on a plan to cover up my wrongdoing.

Staying calm, I closed the freezer. I dried off the ice pick and placed it carefully back in the drawer, just as I had found it. I walked out of the kitchen to the far end of the dining area like nothing had happened. Then I hit the "reset" button. Turning around, I headed back toward the kitchen as if I was clueless. I was humming to myself, strolling nonchalantly, wandering "innocently" toward the freezer. When I opened the door, I discovered a terrible sound! I bent my head near and listened for a moment. What was that? Boldly, I decided I'd better inform my mom quickly that something was wrong with the freezer! I went to her right away to let her know what I had encountered.

My cool manner had not fooled her. I would have to wait for Dad to get home because I was in big trouble now! Tragically, the fridge and freezer unit breathed its last that day. All our cold foods had to be transferred to an ice chest. I'm sure I got an awful spanking that evening. I might remember the actual one!

But the most chilling memory I have, after my premeditated lie was exposed, is the repetitive sight of that tall white appliance sitting lifeless on the cement patio out back. It took days, if not weeks, until my parents could obtain an expensive replacement. Over and over, when I went outside to play or do my chores, I would encounter that dead fridge. My careless and severe disobedience had taught me a grave lesson, that the wages of sin are truly death.

Proverbs 12:22 *"Lying lips are an abomination to the Lord, But those who deal faithfully are His delight."*

Proverbs 15:2-3 *"The tongue of the wise makes knowledge acceptable, But the mouth of fools spouts folly. The eyes of the Lord are in every place, Watching the evil and the good."*

3 YOU SHALL NOT STEAL

As a missionary kid in Tegucigalpa, Honduras I attended a K-12 Mennonite Christian school called Los Pinares. Every weekday morning, the principal, Mr. Jerry Berkey, arrived in front of my house with the long yellow school bus. As the air brakes hissed, and the bus came to a stop, his hand would pull the silver handle and the tall yellow doors with rounded windows and black rubber edges would swish wide open.

From the cement curb, I would climb three steps into the entry and turn near his padded seat. After a shy "Hi," I'd walk along the aisle to choose an open space on a rigid vinyl-covered bench without seat belts. I could enjoy chatting with a schoolmate or join everyone in singing. *The Wheels on the Bus, 99 Bottles of Coke*, and *Don't Throw Your Trash in My Back Yard*, were popular tunes. Many times, I would just sit quietly and think. I liked contemplating in communion with God.

We'd climb out of the city into the mountains on a two-lane road without guard rails. As the way grew narrow, I loved leaning my head on the window, staring out at the alarming descent close beside us. The vibration of the engine tickled my forehead, and the bumpety-bump of the tires jostled my body. The steep hillside was bursting with sky-high pines and low scattered brush. Sunlight and shadows danced alternately on the glass as we passed green, brown, and beige foliage.

THE JOY WEAVER - GRASSROOTS

After a forty-five-minute ride from home, the bus would emerge from the shaded windy road into bright open sky glorying over a beautifully rustic school in a massive clearing on our left. Driving beside the long, barbed-wire fence would lead to the far end of campus. We'd turn left onto a dirt driveway, pull through the arched gateway, and come to a stop near the running track. Time to get off!

I attended two and a half years at Los Pinares with MK friends of all ages. My babysitter, Peter Clark, my wanna-be beau, Abner Reyes, and my best friend, Esther Clark, were all there. I learned the seven colors of God's beautiful rainbow with the acronym ROY G BIV. We grew carrots and radishes in the garden that we could eat and skipped rope in the pavilion.

On track and field days I was fast! I loved to run and earned a large collection of ribbons. Dad would often film me racing with his Super 8mm. Though I disliked cafeteria banana bread, earned a C in Spanish from Mrs. Hess, and once sat crying on the playground sidewalk due to a horrible earache, I remember most of my days there as something of a grand adventure.

But one fateful day, I faced a temptation that would teach me an additional valuable lesson. Our kindergarten teacher provided materials with which to amuse ourselves during free time. They were meant to be kept in the classroom, of course.

On the way home from school that afternoon, I was standing in the bus aisle holding onto a pole as we traveled (since the seats were all full). My classmate showed me playdough he had taken from class and was offering me some! My stomach was queasy. I'm sure I did not say yes right away. I knew full well not to steal. But due to some faulty logic, I rationalized accepting half of it. After all, *I* wasn't the one who had stolen it!

When I got home, my mind was racing. How could I explain

possession of this playdough? I grabbed a Golden Arches Bible story from the rec room bookshelf and hid the soft glob in the middle toward the center. The pages on the top half drooped loosely over the conspicuous lump. Since hiding it wasn't a promising option, I proudly took the playdough to Mom. With tremendous wit (or dastardly stupidity) I had imagined the clever plot in the blink of an eye. "Look what I won as a prize for singing a song in school today!" Oh my…not again!

I stood by Mom's and Dad's bedside enduring invasive questioning. I learned the definition of "accomplice" as conviction pricked my soul. Then came the worst part. In that guilty moment, I wish my parents had just spanked me! Though I did get spanked, I was also told to return the playdough, tell my teacher what I had done, and apologize. It would be HUMILIATING!

It was hard to fall asleep that night. Next morning, I was dreading it. Sitting at my desk I was miserable. My classmates sat so close! It would be best for me to hurry and get it over with. As soon as it seemed possible, I raised my hand during seatwork. My heart was pounding inside my chest as the teacher approached.

She leaned over kindly as I whispered near her ear, "I took this playdough yesterday, and I need to give it back." She took it from my hand and simply said, "Thank you." I squirmed as she began to walk away, knowing that my assigned task was incomplete. Before she had gone too far, I blurted out, "I'm sorry!" With a huge sigh of relief, it was finally over. I was free again! I had suffered the consequences of being mischievous. And I knew I never wanted to experience that kind of embarrassment again!

Exodus 20:15 *"You shall not steal."*

Proverbs 20:11 *"It is by his deeds that a lad distinguishes himself If his conduct is pure and right."*

4 MORNING GLORY

Like every human being, and as observed in the previous two stories, I was born with a sinful nature. Mom tells about a couple of times I ignored her stern warning, "Don't touch." Once, I stuck my hand into the freshly sprayed oven cleaner. Another time, I plopped right down in the sticky black tar on the newly paved road in front of our house. (Dad had to come from work and help Mom clean my tender toddler skin with a harsh product.)

I regularly snuck into the outdoor shed to crunch dry, savory dog food. And peeing in the public swimming pool was way more convenient than heading to the restroom. Once I "ran away" after setting a note on the dining table. Instead of leaving, I had climbed into a 50-gallon drum in the living room. I stifled my giggles, listening to my parents read the note and wonder where I'd gone.

My little brother suffered much due to my rascally nature. I often instigated things that got us in trouble or caused him grief. The Hotel Maya pool was a favorite place for us to go, with Mom or as a family, or with friends. One afternoon there, John and I started chasing each other on the pool deck around the deep end. I ducked when passing under the diving board, but he did not. He slammed into it, fell back, and started to bleed. After a lot of fuss over his wounded forehead, he was taken to get stitches. I sat pondering among empty chairs at a table by the pool. We had come as a group, so I wasn't alone.

Nancy McComb

One time I scribbled in pen on a plush jewelry box that Mom had given John, and not me. When he tattled, I refused to confess. We were made to sit on a long table in his room for time-out until one of us owned up. Out of Mom's earshot, I told him I was not going to give in. Many long minutes later he "confessed" and accepted a spanking, just to be done with it! What a stinky sister! Even worse, I listened to him getting punished and congratulated myself for having won the ordeal and escaped.

The first indication of my spiritual renewal came one Sunday morning in the spring when I was six years old. I was walking blissfully one foot in front of the other on a garden wall in my beautiful dress before church. I felt the smiling presence of God as the sun rose brilliantly, climbing above the horizon. Did I know that He was coming for me? Did I have any inkling about the crazy love He had to pour into my needy heart? *I was like a shriveled morning glory lifting its head, spreading its petals to meet the warm caress of dawn's first light.* But did I know how much my sin had grieved Him? Did I know my sin had cost God's Son his life?

My Sunday School teacher was sharing the Easter story later in a rear classroom of Union Christian Church. Heavenly Father's Holy Spirit was pressing on my conscience with a deep sense of weighty responsibility for wrongs I had done. *There came a chilling awareness of the cost of my sin, like the brisk breath of daybreak when that first sliver of morning challenges the night.* I could be so naughty. Lectures and spankings were something I encountered often.

I knew I needed a Savior. *My soul was awakening with a deep desire for salvation, like petals thirsting for the sunbeams of forgiveness and redemption.* I didn't pray right then, and I don't even remember if we were invited to do so. I went home and talked to Mom.

My parents' bedroom was a familiar scene. A bad dream or nausea in the night could propel me there from my room across the hall. My parents would rouse sleepily to offer comfort or support. Or John and I would snuggle on each side of Mom as she read us books like *Santa Mouse* or *The Chronicles of Narnia*. At the worst of times, I would be looking up into one of their stern faces as they sat on the edge of the bed, looking down at me, standing on the floor rug. This usually meant a speech before a spanking.

This Sunday afternoon was different. Mom was asking questions to see if I understood the decision I wanted to make. "Why do you want to ask Jesus into your heart?" "Can you explain what He did so you could be saved?" When she was assured by my kindergarten answers, it was time to pray.

Where does a short kid go to get down on her knees? We got up, and I walked into the ensuite bathroom. There was a perfect place for me to kneel! I bent down on the floor rug by Mom's squeaky-clean toilet, leaned my elbows on the carpeted lid, bowed my head in my hands, and waited for Mom to lead. She said a prayer for me to repeat, and I invited Jesus into my life.

"Dear Jesus, I know I'm a sinner. I'm sorry for the wrong things I've done. I know you're perfect and can't allow sinners into heaven. I believe you are God's Son. I believe you died on the cross to take the punishment for my sins. Please forgive me and come into my heart as my Savior. I know you rose again and give me eternal life. Thank you for making me part of your forever family! In Jesus' Name, Amen."

In that moment, the Holy Spirit of Jesus came in! I could feel His presence. I could tell my life was different! I was my Beloved's, and He was mine. His banner over me was love! *My heart had opened wide and free, like the Morning Glory flower in full bloom. I was fully confident under His bright gaze, unashamed in my Father's world. I felt beautiful, lovingly clothed in a robe of purple velvet, brushed with strokes of glistening white: royal!* I was so excited that I shared the good news with my brother using felt characters on a flannelgraph board in the rec room. John accepted Jesus as His Savior, too. He was only four years old!

John 3:16 *"For God so loved the world, that He gave His only begotten Son, that whoever believes in Him shall not perish, but have eternal life."*

Romans 10:9 *"...if you confess with your mouth Jesus as Lord, and believe in your heart that God raised Him from the dead, you will be saved;"*

5 GOLDEN RAG MEMORIES

Mountains were tall and majestic,
studded with towering pines
in the beautiful land of Honduras
where it was sunny most of the time.

The country was brimming with culture –
from carved Mayan idols to oil paintings
of adobe-walled, red-roofed houses
and native women carrying baskets of things.

Banana plantations were everywhere
filling the countryside,
and coffee too was grown down there.
It had become a national pride.

Though the country was gorgeous and golden
from the Spanish way of life,
poverty touched most of the lives
of every niñito, man and wife.

The shacks were scattered by the riverside
like boxes thrown away.
And women knelt to scrub their rags-
put them on rocks so they'd dry out that day.

Sometimes it would rain and pour
and the shanties would go down,

Nancy McComb

crushed by the mighty, muddy river that roared,
unaware of the people it drowned.

The beggar kids were all around
with soiled faces and big brown eyes.
They blew their noses onto the ground;
they always drew the flies.

They carried plastic garbage bags
and went from door to door,
standing there in piteous rags,
saying, "somos pobres," ("we are poor").

Some beggars were very old
with thin gray hair and wrinkled skin.
They'd ask, "Me das dinero?"
with gummy toothless grins.

One day just such a man came by,
and clanging on our fence,
asked for money to buy food,
maybe a lempira? (worth 50 cents)

I shook my head from left to right,
and quietly he went on.
His retreating figure - such a sight.
Well, soon he would be gone.

THE JOY WEAVER - GRASSROOTS

But guilt began to stir inside.
My stomach was in knots.
Down my cheeks, tears started to slide.
I ran into the house.

I brought out my little piggy bank
and looked way down the street.
But the cringy man was almost gone,
hobbling away on sore bare feet.

These memories will remain always.
I saw both sides of life.
I'm glad I spent my younger days
learning of many peoples' strife.

Now when I see someone in need,
I'll be more inclined not to turn away;
but somehow do just my small part
to help them see another day.

© September 30, 1985 Nancy

6 MISSION TRANSITION

The summer I was 8, my family packed our prized possessions in 50-gallon drums, cleaned out the house in Tegucigalpa and left the most significant place my brother and I had ever called home. Crazy, because we were not even sure where we would end up! Our first plan of action was to drive across the United States for a couple of months, visiting relatives, old friends, and supporting churches. Dad's slide show would be projected over and over, telling the story of what God had been doing in Honduras.

Mom and Dad had gone to Honduras as newlyweds, and great developments had been made in the radio ministry during the eleven years they served. HRVC's broadcast of the Good News into Honduras, other parts of Central America, and beyond had improved. Dad's primary responsibility as Chief Engineer had been to maintain the radio transmitter site. This included the transmitter equipment in a small cement-block building built into the steep, rocky, grass-carpeted hillside, an extended short-wave antenna strung between buildings, and the huge radio tower. That soaring spire of steel rose into the sky, secured by guy wires. If the red lamp on top went out, Dad had to climb up and change it! At times, if the radio station went off air after hours, Dad would get a call at home to come fix it, even if it was dinner time!

Through the years, Honduran staff had grown skilled enough to manage the station on their own. Their godly character, technical training, and financial stability qualified them to carry the radio ministry forward with success. Like parents celebrate when their kids grow up and prosper independently, missionaries get excited to give ownership and administration of mission projects to national leaders!

But what would Dad do next? Radio engineering was not a typical ministry project for our mission. Where would they use a man (and his family) with those skills? To me, the mystery of an unknown future was exciting. I was safe in my parents' care. They had consistently modeled unwavering faith in God. They believed the Lord had a plan and trusted He would help us figure it out. I was aware that one of the possibilities would be leaving our mission organization. But I also knew that our mission leaders were hoping to find a new assignment for us. We would all keep prayerfully seeking an answer and wait for God's guidance.

So off we went to "home assignment" in the U.S. We lived in a furnished brick duplex on the parking lot of the First Baptist church in Wayne, Michigan. This became home base while we visited relatives, gave reports of our missions work to churches and supporters, attended mission meetings and trainings, visited doctors, and set up our tent in campgrounds across Michigan. Our car traveled many miles that summer!

While driving down a highway or navigating through the streets, we would search for all 50 state license plates. When traveling long distance, Dad would position cans of Spaghetti-O's on our car's engine block to heat as we drove. Sooner or later, we'd hit a rest stop. Mom would serve the hot pasta on paper plates with other tasty foods. Cheap roadside lunches were the best!

Brilliantly lit, spiffy clean stores created a new sense of wanting. There were cool city Lego sets with cars and people, and real-looking dolls that drank bottles and dirtied diapers. There were Hot Wheels cars with loopty-loop racetracks, yarn and bead crafts, hip new clothes, and fancy foods preserved in bags, boxes, and cans.

I had loved my life in Honduras. I also loved life in the U.S. Looking similar to everyone else was a new kind of familiar and comfortable. Houses had attics and basements, with that strong smell of America: generations of goods stored away, infiltrated by the humidity of spring rain, hot summer, misty fall, and winter snow. Those seasons were fun to play in, too! I could swim in an above-ground pool, jump in a leaf pile, build a snow fort, sled down icy white hills, and warm up with hot cocoa!

And I loved the thunder of a train rolling by, hollering with its whistle. Train tracks ran atop a berm behind the chain-link fence surrounding the back yard of our duplex. But if the train blew by while I was trying to watch Kaptain Kangaroo on American T.V., I would miss part of the story. That was frustrating because you could not rewind a program back in those days!

One day I discovered a snapping turtle in the tall grass just outside our back door. It was by the coiled green hose, just under the faucet secured to our brick wall. Maybe the black and yellow reptile had come looking for water. My parents let me keep *Snapper* for a while. I learned to guard my fingers from its sharp snout when giving it little chunks of raw meat! And watching him do life was fun. Sooner or later, I let him lumber back to freedom.

I enjoyed riding my bike around the empty church parking lot in front of our house. But one day, as I was speeding along, I collided with Uncle Eric's dog, Kia. In that shocking moment, she yelped and lept away while I flew over the handlebars to be decorated with raspberries. We were dog sitting at the time, so I

THE JOY WEAVER - GRASSROOTS

phoned Uncle Eric to profusely apologize! He was kind, and thankfully, pregnant Kia was not hurt.

Another day playing in the empty lot, I was having a literal ball with the colorful orb my parents had let me buy at the missionary happy land, Kmart. It was a BIG ball, and bouncing it made me really happy. Unfortunately, I was also holding a long stick with sharp protrusions where branches had been snapped off. I knew that batting the ball with it was risky but failed to consider the consequences of my poor judgment. I gripped the stick firmly in my hand, stubbornly determined that I would hit the ball only with the smooth places, and not the poky places.

Suddenly, my prized Kmart special burst in a body-shivering "Pop!" I was crushed. Why did I have to learn the hard way sometimes? I spent a long time in my room shedding crocodile tears. Mom realized my lament had shifted to grieving all the people I had left behind in Honduras. Transition was a lot of fun in some ways. But I had also said good-bye to most of my "lifelong" friends and might never see them again. Mom comforted me, and my sorrows began to subside. We might have even prayed together about making new friends in our next place.

By summer's end, my parents had an inkling of what our next post would be. It was time to depart from Michigan and head to California. While we awaited an official decision from the mission, my parents moved forward by faith that God would complete the process He had begun. If plans were approved, we would fly to a tropical paradise where Dad could use his radio skills in a new assignment.

All our belongings, many of them never unpacked since leaving Honduras, were loaded on a truck headed for a shipyard out west. Meanwhile, the four of us loaded up our car and headed for the coast. I will never forget days later, standing in the shallow end of a sun-kissed pool at an affordable hotel. Coming from a phone call that had been answered inside the lobby, Mom burst through the sliding glass doors to the pool deck. She exclaimed, "Are you ready to move to Hawaii?!"

"Yes!" I cheered. Life was taking on a whole new flavor.

Psalm 143:8 *"Let me hear Your lovingkindness in the morning; For I trust in You; Teach me the way in which I should walk; For to You I lift up my soul."*

Romans 8:14 *"For all who are being led by the Spirit of God, these are the sons of God."*

7 A FIRM FOUNDATION

I grew up in a strong Christian home. Mind you, I did not say perfect. Nonetheless, Mom and Dad took their parenting responsibilities seriously. They knew God's Word instilled them with parental authority. God's Word, the Bible, provided the source of all wisdom with which to do their best at discipling and disciplining my younger brother and me. We were raised with the awareness of God's presence and love, the truth of God's Word, the conviction of our sins, and the priority of being ambassadors for Christ to people who had not yet heard of or believed in Him.

Proverbs 22:6 *"Train up a child in the way he should go, Even when he is old he will not depart from it."*

Proverbs 9:10 *"The fear of the Lord is the beginning of wisdom, And the knowledge of the Holy One is understanding."*

Hebrews 12:8-11 *"But if you are without discipline, of which all have become partakers, then you are illegitimate children and not sons. Furthermore, we had earthly fathers to discipline us, and we respected them; shall we not much rather be subject to the Father of spirits, and live? For they disciplined us for a short time as seemed best to them, but He disciplines us for our good, so that we may share His holiness. All discipline for the moment seems not to be joyful, but sorrowful; yet to those who have been trained by it, afterwards it yields the peaceful fruit of righteousness."*

Proverbs 1:8-9 *"Hear, my son, your father's instruction, And do not forsake your mother's teaching; Indeed, they are a graceful wreath to your head, And ornaments about your neck."*

Training my brother and me right from wrong did not keep us from sinning; but it did guard us from thinking that sin was harmless. One day at a time, our parents used Biblical truth to train us to be sensitive to the Holy Spirit. And discipline was not meant to be painless! It taught us that sin *causes* pain.

A spanking, alone time, or loss of privileges instilled in us the realization that sin is costly and uncomfortable. Temporary benefits or pleasures of wrongdoing would not be worth the physical, social, psychological, and spiritual consequences to ourselves or those we influenced. On the other hand, our choices to obey would bring blessing and peace to ourselves and those around us.

Proverbs 22:15 *"Foolishness is bound up in the heart of a child; The rod of discipline will remove it far from him."*

Romans 3:23 *"for all have sinned and fall short of the glory of God,"*

Deuteronomy 11:18-19 *"You shall therefore impress these words of mine on your heart and on your soul; and you shall bind them as a sign on your hand, and they shall be as frontals on your forehead. You shall teach them to your sons, talking of them when you sit in your house and when you walk along the road and when you lie down and when you rise up."*

One way we obeyed God's Word as a family was by attending church. At church we met with believing friends to hear messages from God's Word, worship God and pray. Church meetings, service projects and fun church family activities gave us the chance to talk and bond with likeminded people. We helped each other grow in our walks with Jesus. And we challenged each other to tell people about Jesus.

Leviticus 19:3 *"Every one of you shall reverence his mother and his father, and you shall keep My sabbaths; I am the LORD your God."*

I Timothy 4:13 *"Until I come, give attention to the public reading of Scripture, to exhortation and teaching."*

Colossians 3:16 *"Let the word of Christ richly dwell within you, with all wisdom teaching and admonishing one another with psalms and hymns and spiritual songs, singing with thankfulness in your hearts to God."*

Hebrews 10:24-25 *"and let us consider how to stimulate one another to love and good deeds, not forsaking our own assembling together, as is the habit of some, but encouraging one another; and all the more, as you see the day drawing near."*

Matthew 28:19-20 *"Go therefore and make disciples of all the nations, baptizing them in the name of the Father and the Son and the Holy Spirit, teaching them to observe all that I commanded you;"*

Sunday school was a fun place to memorize verses. We had contests and received prizes. We learned the shortest chapter in the Bible, Psalm 100. We learned the Shepherd's Psalm 23. We learned about spiritual protection and spiritual warfare from Ephesians 6:10-18, the gospel from John 3:16-18, the meaning of true love from 1 Corinthians 13, and the truth about the Creation of the world in Genesis 1.

Psalm 19:8 *"The precepts of the LORD are right, rejoicing the heart; The commandment of the LORD is pure, enlightening the eyes."*

Nancy McComb

Psalm 119:11 *"Your word I have treasured in my heart, That I may not sin against You."*

Psalm 119:105 *"Your word is a lamp to my feet, And a light to my path."*

At nine years old, my pastor at International Baptist Church (IBC) in Honolulu, Hawaii was Dr. James R. Cook, a descendant of the explorer, Captain James Cook, one of the first outsiders to discover the Hawaiian Islands. Pastor Jim had been an MK in India. He was proud of his heritage and deeply loved Jesus. I firmly respected him. Besides, his missionary stories were inspiring. One time, he had accompanied his sick mother to the U.S. by train and boat, on his own at age 13! I thought he was amazing.

Jim Cook's father also served in ministry at our church. Grand Pastor, as we called him, was a regal man of sweet disposition with bright white hair. Pastor Jim had wavy silver hair, and an authoritative presence with an equally warm glow. And he held women in high regard. Every time a woman came on stage, the men on stage stood to honor her. He was publicly sweet on his wife, Shirley. We loved her, too. She was as excellent as he was.

Pastor Him also fostered family fun in our congregation. We were constantly enjoying family picnics, family camps, and special concerts and activities.

I began scribbling notes from his vibrant sermons in third grade, shortly after we started attending. Much of my early loyalty and respect for Jesus was fostered by Pastor Jim's reverence for Scripture, his interesting testimonies, his firm and fun personality, and his clear expectations of godly living.

Hebrews 13:7 *"Remember those who led you, who spoke the word of God to you; and considering the result of their conduct, imitate their faith."*

Ephesians 4:11-13 *"And He gave some as apostles, and some as prophets, and some as evangelists, and some as pastors and teachers, for the equipping of the saints for the work of service, to the building up of the body of Christ; until we all attain to the unity of the faith, and of the knowledge of the Son of God, to a mature man, to the measure of the stature which belongs to the fullness of Christ."*

Regarding Christ's crucifixion, Pastor Jim made sure we did not take our salvation for granted. He read vivid descriptions of Jesus' immense sufferings as He was wounded for our transgressions. Sticky spit was hurled at Him in disgust from haters whom He would shed His blood for. Torturous lashes from the "cat of nine tails," (leather straps with shards of metal and glass) ripped His flesh forty times as He knelt innocent before His punishers.

Passion Week reenactments displayed graphic sights and sounds. We saw and heard the thundering blows from the hammers pounding on the nails that pierced His wrists and ankles. And the sorrows of His heart were evident when some of those He was dying for carelessly bartered for His clothing.

I could imagine the crown of thorns jammed harshly on His head, sharply digging into His skin. There should have been a gleaming crown of gold honorably placed there. Instead, they yelled at Him, humiliated Him, mocked His royalty, and crucified Him. They gave Him vinegar when He was thirsty. They watched the perfect Son of the Living God die a criminal's death.

I would often lament with tears during quiet prayer time, as if I had been there in Jerusalem that week. I knew I could have been one of His accusers: clueless, selfish, and stubborn. I knew my sins were part of the reason He had chosen to die, to take my punishment on Himself, and give His life in exchange for mine.

On the first Sunday of every month, we did not take communion lightly. In fact, I did not take communion at all until after I was baptized at age 10. Pastor Jim's firm grip had plunged me charismatically into the small square pool outdoors after pronouncing, "I baptize you in the name of the Father, the Son, and the Holy Spirit." Down under the water I went, symbolizing death to my old ways. Out of the water I came, embodying Christ's resurrection in a public display of commitment to walk with Jesus daily.

Acts 19:4 *"Paul said, 'John baptized with the baptism of repentance, telling the people to believe in Him who was coming after him, that is, in Jesus.'"*

Romans 6:4 *"Therefore we have been buried with Him through baptism into death, so that as Christ was raised from the dead through the glory of the Father, so we too might walk in newness of life."*

I Corinthians 11:26 *"For as often as you eat this bread and drink the cup, you proclaim the Lord's death until He comes."*

Observing the sacraments of baptism and communion as a church family taught me at a young age to relish confession and repentance as valuable gifts! Admitting my sins out loud was always hard but brought me relief. Sometimes I confessed quickly, and sometimes it took years to speak up. Each time I confessed, I was freed from guilt and shame. This allowed me to experience joy in honest relationships with nothing to hide.

Proverbs 28:13 *"He who conceals his transgressions will not prosper, But he who confesses and forsakes them will find compassion."*

James 5:16 *"Therefore, confess your sins to one another, and pray for one another so that you may be healed.*

1 John 1:9 *"If we confess our sins, He is faithful and righteous to forgive us our sins and to cleanse us from all unrighteousness."*

Psalm 103:8-12 *"The Lord is compassionate and gracious, Slow to anger and abounding in lovingkindness. He will not always strive with us, Nor will He keep His anger forever. He has not dealt with us according to our sins, Nor rewarded us according to our iniquities. For as high as the heavens are above the earth, So great is His lovingkindness toward those who fear Him. As far as the east is from the west, So far has He removed our transgressions from us."*

And that was just the beginning! My parents' investment in Bible-based child-rearing with love and prayer was the best gift they will have ever given me. God's nourishing Word was crucial in developing a sturdy intellectual foundation, a vibrant emotional health, and a dynamic process of spiritual growth. Dad's and Mom's examples of serving the Lord in ministry and prioritizing obedience to God according to His Word in daily life was effectively compelling and contagious.

Psalm 119:9-10 *"How can a young man keep his way pure? By keeping it according to Your word. With all my heart I have sought You; Do not let me wander from Your commandments."*

Romans 12:2 *"And do not be conformed to this world, but be transformed by the renewing of your mind, so that you may prove what the will of God is, that which is good and acceptable and perfect."*

Psalm 119:5 *"Oh that my ways may be established, To keep Your statutes!"*

These grassroot principles harvested from the firm foundation of God's Word, handed down generation to generation, would provide the framework of faith in which to grow as a genuine follower of Jesus Christ throughout the rest of my life. It is amazing to me that this invisible, intangible framework could produce life with so much safety and security in an atmosphere of ongoing creativity and joy!

8 ALOHA

Oahu, Hawaii was more like a foreign land than part of America. The flight from Los Angeles to Honolulu lasted five hours over ocean! We exited the plane and proceeded through balmy open-air walkways. The peculiar nature of this place was immediately evident. Where else in America did men wear necklaces called *leis*, made of fragrant living flowers? Where else in America did women wear dresses called *muumuus*, like nightgowns more than day wear? Public restrooms were labeled *kane* and *wahine*. Thank you signs in the airport read, "*Mahalo nui loa.*" This was a remarkable state. Michigan was the only other state I had lived in!

At the time we arrived, Hawaii had been the U.S. flag's 50th star for only eighteen years. Queen Liliu'okalani, the last reigning monarch of the Kingdom of Hawaii, had been deceased for only 60 years.[3] The USS Arizona Memorial (commemorating lives lost in the surprise attack on Pearl Harbor on December 7, 1941) had only been standing over the watery grave, with 1102 sailors and Marines still buried inside, for 15 years.[4]

Iolani Palace, the King Kamehameha statue and the Pali Lookout vividly depicted scenes of the former kingdom's power. The Aiea Loop Trail wound past the remains of a Japanese airplane crashed during World War II. The Stairway to Heaven, or Haiku Stairs, built by the Navy in 1942, was and is a series of almost four thousand stair and ladder steps climbing 2000 ft. above sea level and along the Ko'olau mountain ridges.[5] On top was an old, abandoned transmitter station. (*When I hiked there in high school with my youth group, I was told it was there that incoming Japanese aircraft had been spotted by radar and assumed to be B-17's on December 7, 1941. I've since read that the real visual interception took place elsewhere.*[6])

Hawaiian culture saturated everyday life. The official State song, "Hawaii Pono'i" had been written by King David Kalakaua in 1876, in honor of King Kamehameha I, who had founded the former Hawaiian Kingdom in 1810.[7] We sang it often.

Our state fish was the humuhumunukunukuapua'a. We could lay eyes on it through our snorkeling masks while swimming over the coral reefs in Hanauma Bay. Every public-school elementary kid learned to play the ukulele in music class. And street signs could be challenging to read without a phonics lesson in Hawaiian. The phonetic Hawaiian alphabet only has 13 letters; and the 5 vowels are used prolifically!

Tourist attractions provided us with an inside look at the local culture of which we were becoming a part. The Polynesian Cultural Center demonstrated integral facets of Polynesian life such as various games played with stringed pompoms and the long-haul seaworthy design of outrigger canoes. Hawaiians were descendants of the Polynesians.

Tropical dancers in the Kodak Hula Show performed all the island styles while bare-chested men with palm-frond crowns kept rhythm on loud gourd drums. A luau on the beach lit by tiki torches would feature tropical fruits, roasted pig and purple-paste poi (from taro root).

Huffing and puffing up the arduous trail inside of Diamond Head crater would grant a view of the sparkling coastline from inside the iconic bulkhead seen on so many Waikiki Beach postcards. In ancient times, this massive crater had been formed by the fervor of a volcanic explosion. There are 8 primary Hawaiian islands, Oahu being the principle one. The biggest one is called Hawaii, or the Big Island. There are 137 total islands in the chain!

The terrain of the islands was gorgeous. I would never take for granted the sheer beauty of lush green volcanically formed mountain ranges, cascading waterfalls, and sparkling blue seas kissing 227 miles of Oahu coastline - even as an eventual fourteen-year *kama'aina* resident. Steep mountain trails, cliff jumps into chilly water holes, dark damp lava tubes, palm tree branches twirling with the stars in the moonlight, a coastal ocean geyser called the Blowhole, skilled surfers on the North Shore, shaved ice snack shacks, sticky rice and fried chicken shops, aloha shirts and flip-flops, and slack-key guitar were all vibing island life.

International Baptist Church (IBC) was nestled within the velvety green foothills of the Ko'olau Mountain Range in Nuuanu Valley, on the Pali Highway descending into the leeward side of the island. Hilly streets in the area wound through thickly populated neighborhoods, past historical residences, into parking lots of high rises, next to churches and lavishly ornate temples.

Native Hawaiians had been practicing polytheism and animism for millennia, worshiping, fearing, and placating troublesome spirits. Eastern religions like Taoism, Shintoism and Buddhism dominated the culture in this unique United States mid-Pacific outpost between North America and Asia.

Christians were a minute part of the population, just 1% according to surveys at the time. Yet unfortunately, some of my parents' supporters dropped their financial partnership due to our vacationland assignment. It was hard for them to see that a tropical paradise could be a viable mission field in need of the gospel.

The near absence of Biblical proclamation and Christian discipleship in the islands was the very reason that radio station, 95.5 KAIM, had been established. Billy Graham's Christian Broadcasting Association had put the station on the air in 1953.[8] Now there were several engineering projects planned that would upgrade their broadcasting capabilities.[9] So KAIM gladly "borrowed" my dad from the Conservative Baptist Home Mission Society to serve as an engineer. Our family was settling in for a long while.

Psalm 97:1 *"The Lord reigns, let the earth rejoice; Let the many islands be glad."*

Isaiah 42:10 *"Sing to the Lord a new song, Sing His praise from the end of the earth! You who go down to the sea, and all that is in it. You islands, and those who dwell on them."*

9 THE 30-DAY CHALLENGE

While John and I were in second and third grades, our sibling rivalry grew out of hand. We argued all the time, and sometimes hit or smacked each other. It is true that we had endured intense transition for more than a year – from Honduras to Michigan to Hawaii, with many road trips in between. Arriving in Hawaii, we had lived short-term in a rental house in Kailua and attended Kailua Elementary school. A few months later we moved to our first-ever purchased home in Kaneohe and switched to Aikahi Elementary. Yet all that moving was no excuse for nastiness. We all needed to have some fun! My parents tirelessly insisted that we get along. And still, we fought!

The Bible's instructions about how parents should discipline their kids are more principle-based than precisely prescriptive. What is Biblically imperative is that parents do manage to train their children in the ways of the Lord, and not lose their cool while doing it! In the early years we had been accustomed to stern warnings or spankings. As we got older, "time out" or loss of privileges were commonly used for reasoning with us. Lately, Mom had resorted to making us stand face to face and hold hands until we could apologize and ask each other's forgiveness.

John and I were sibling rivals and great friends simultaneously. I remember one playtime as little kids in Honduras. We had built a long, divided highway in the middle of our hallway. We used square letter blocks as the median. And then we pushed toy cars back and forth for hours on the cement tile floor. Driving was fun!

We loved road trips. One summer our family had driven a Ford Taunus up the Pan American highway to the U.S. for home assignment. Seatbelts were not required in those days, so Dad had built us an activity platform that was set over top of the luggage in the hatchback. My brother and I could read books, play games, or sleep if we wanted.

Whether we were playing cars at home or riding in a real car, or doing anything else together, eventually we would fight about space, or possessions or the rules of play. As stated, not long after moving to Hawaii, my brother and I were bickering, worse than ever. And no matter what Mom and Dad tried, our enmities would flare up in the simplest of scenarios. Unless my parents could get ahold of our hearts, minds, and wills for cooperation, the battle was going to rage on endlessly.

And then Mom received an inspiration. We all loved ice cream. We loved trying the 31 flavors of Baskin Robbins when coupons came in the newspaper. We loved cheap vanilla soft-serve cones from McDonald's and noted which server made the tallest stack of swirls. Dad could eat a half-gallon of chocolate chip mint if no one stopped him. And I was to become a midnight ice cream thief during high school. Ice cream was a sure way to lure us toward behavior modification!

Mom sat my brother and me down, "All right you two, your fights are driving your dad and me crazy! The arguing must stop. I'm offering each of you a Baskin-Robbins seven-scoop

Matterhorn Sundae, with all the toppings you want, if you're able to go thirty days without a single argument."

John and I looked at each other with wide eyes and big-open mouths, then turned to Mom with gleeful grins. "You've got a deal!" we agreed. It is whimsical how that challenge elated us, bonded us together, made us say silly nice things to each other, scoot out of each other's way, and refuse to fight about anything! 1, 2, 3, 4, 5, 6, 7. Days were passing slowly by, but soon we'd kept the peace a whole week!

Finally, after more than four weeks, we had arrived near the finish line. It was the evening of the 29th day, and we only had to behave one more day! All four of us had gotten in the car to go somewhere, maybe Wednesday night church. There was an umbrella in the back seat between us, and I got annoyed. I shoved it toward John. Then John got annoyed and pushed it toward me. Then I said, "It belongs on your side!" and knocked it to the floor. He retorted, "No, it belongs on your side!"

Suddenly, Mom turned around from the passenger seat and looked at us alarmingly. We looked back at her in suspended silence…and then began to plead. "No, Mom! Come on! We're so close! We hardly argued! You can't count that against us!"

What is a mother to do? She and Dad thought about it and talked it over quietly. We sat there wallowing in grievous remorse, waiting to hear our fate. Finally, she said, "All right. This is what Dad and I have decided. Since you've done so well until now, we are just going to add an extra day. If you can get to the end of day thirty-one without another argument, you'll still earn your ice cream."

I'm thankful to say the grace card worked! We hunkered down for the last couple of days before being awarded our coveted treat. I can still see myself sitting there with my family at a small round table in Baskin-Robbins. John and I were each savoring our colossal seven-scoop Matterhorn Sundaes with sticky toppings, and whipped cream, and nuts, and a cherry on top! Mom's "get along" challenge had worked, and my parents' wise discipline had never tasted so good!

Proverbs 19:20 *"Listen to counsel and accept discipline, That you may be wise the rest of your days."*

Hebrews 12:11 *"All discipline for the moment seems not to be joyful...yet to those who have been trained by it... it yields the peaceful fruit of righteousness."*

10 A NEW CREATION

Third grade through sixth grade I attended public school at Aikahi Elementary in Kaneohe, Hawaii. My classmates were *keikis* from all over the world: Japan, China, Korea, Thailand, Laos, Polynesia, Vietnam, India, Portugal, Great Britain, and of course Hawaii. Caucasians mixed with other races were called *hapa*. They were the most beautiful. For some reason, racial playground jokes usually picked on the Polish. On "kill *haole* day" a brown-skinned local boy named Kaleo planned to throw eggs at us white kids. It was amusing because most of us got along fine.

Pidgin English impregnated our conversations with island zest. "Aloooo-ha!" "Eh, bradda!" "Shaka, bra!" The school lunch menu featured *luau* foods like *lomi-lomi* tomatoes and sticky purple *poi*. Saying *"mahalo"* was exercising your manners; and if you were especially grateful, you said, "Mahalo nui loa!" Heading to the restroom, I knew I was a *wahine* and not a *kane*. *Pakalolo* scent wafting from the school bathroom or lingering on a discarded matchbook was sure trouble.

Home at your *hale*, it was customary to leave footwear on the shoe shelf of the *lanai*. A *malihini* was *akamai* if they caught that cue shortly after arriving in Hawaii. *Ohana* gatherings in tropical December, were especially fun. Mom, Dad, John and I sang "*Mele Kalikimaka*" on a bright Hawaiian Christmas day! And we might call the chief Christmas party planner "The Big *Kahuna*!"

Nancy McComb

Flower *leis*, sold in booths at the airport or floral stores in town, came in dozens of colors, lengths, and smells. This was an essential traditional gift for welcoming new arrivals, celebrating birthdays, saying good-bye, or commemorating graduations. At times, the recipient would be blinded by the lush mane of floral necklaces rising atop their shoulders! Weddings called for costly strands of shiny black kukui nuts for the groom or long strands of delicate white pikake flowers for the bride. As locals, we could string our own *leis* with needle and thread, using neighborhood flowers from Plumeria trees and bougainvillea bushes.

An extensive bougainvillea hedge bordered the entrance to the townhouse complex where I and many friends lived. This wall of luxurious green foliage blossomed repetitively with papery fuchsia blossoms. Each three-petal cluster enrobed a miniature bouquet of itty-bitty white flowers. The bushes came alive with choirs of buzzing bees, each dipping their proboscis into a stamen in search of sweet nectar. But an even bigger gala transpired seasonally when throngs of Painted Lady butterflies or clouds of Kamehameha Pulelehua came flitting and fluttering on the wind to nestle in the branches and sip from the floral nectaries.[10]

One afternoon in fourth grade, neighbor Michelle and I stepped off the City Bus at our stop in front of the bushes. Hundreds of butterflies decorated the entire length of the bougainvillea hedge. We were enamored by the vibrant colors and spirited movements of this cheerful ecosystem. Then one of us got a crazy idea! Since we were both excited about it, Michelle and I ran up the long sidewalk that cut through sprawling lawns and landscape toward our neighboring townhomes. We grabbed large paper grocery sacks and jars before heading back down the hill.

THE JOY WEAVER - GRASSROOTS

With childish pluck and heavy-handed persistence, we captured every butterfly we could manage. We also broke off long poky offshoots with flowers to take with us. After transporting our collections to Michelle's bedroom, we closed the door and scattered the branches across the carpet. Bright sunshine poured in through glass sliders to the balcony. Jar lids came off and bags were opened to release the critters. Michelle's room had been transformed into a beautiful butterfly garden!

Regal winged insects flew about, landed on flowers, investigated the space, or sat there stunned. Some injured ones made us feel sad. We also discovered black ants scurrying, inchworms lurching and moths flitting about in the bougainvillea world! Baby food jar lids held water. I still remember a popular song playing on the FM radio that day. It was the Bee Gees 1977 hit "How Deep Is Your Love." Although it is a secular love song, some of the lyrics mirrored the momentous occasion about to unfold like the dried wings of a butterfly recently emerged from its chrysalis.

"I believe in you. You know the door to my very soul. You're the light in my deepest, darkest hour. You're my savior when I fall.... How deep is your love."

I talked with Michelle that afternoon about how much Jesus loved her, and how He had died on a cross to take the punishment for her sins. I don't know for sure what opened the door for that important talk. Was it the joyful atmosphere of the butterflies?

2 Corinthians 5:17 says, *"Therefore, if anyone is in Christ, there is a new creation; the old things passed away; behold, new things have come."* As a missionary kid attending a public school, sharing the Good News about Jesus was often on my mind. In any case, when I invited her to ask Jesus into her heart, she said "Yes!"

Like my mom had done for me back in kindergarten, I modeled a prayer in short sentences so Michelle could repeat after me one line at a time. We were a bit silly at one point, but I sensed her desire to receive Christ as her Savior was genuine. I've often prayed that Michelle will stand firm in her faith; and I look forward to seeing her in heaven one day!

Romans 10:9-10 *"…if you confess with your mouth Jesus as Lord, and believe in your heart that God raised Him from the dead, you will be saved; for with the heart a person believes, resulting in righteousness, and with the mouth he confesses, resulting in salvation."*

11 UNASHAMED

Aikahi Elementary School in Kaneohe, Hawaii was situated in rows of classrooms located along spacious grass yards. Each time the bell rang, throngs of older students exited the building onto cement-paved, tin-roofed *lanais* outside. I was always glad for a whiff of fresh tropical breeze or a tickle of warmth from refracted sunlight on my outdoors-loving skin. On rainy days we might get splashed by the chilly drops of a downpour just beyond the overhang. Whatever the weather, we would stop at our lockers lining the walkway to chat with friends, grab a snack or pick up supplies for the next subject. Then off we'd go to our next class.

At the front of the school, next to the main entry parking lot, the tree-speckled play area hosted a huge round sand pit. In the center of the deepest sand was a spiraling staircase of giant logs on end, ascending or descending in both directions, from the tallest one in the middle. We amused ourselves endlessly with all sorts of games there.

In one of them, two of us would begin to climb up from opposing directions, and then face off for the challenge at whatever spot we "ran into each other." Each person would pound their closed fist on an open palm in rhythm to the chant, "Junk an' a po! I can no' show!" The one who slapped down the superior hand signal of rock, paper, or scissors on the last word, won that round.

Nancy McComb

The loser retreated a step. The winner advanced. Hit "repeat" until finally, one of us would end up back down in the sand where we had come from. Game over.

Drainage ditches, along one of the sports fields in back, would "erupt" with tiny black toads, just weeks after a heavy rain. Toad eggs that had been laid in the rain puddles, would hatch, and go through metamorphosis, until the little creatures were hopping around the dry ditch by the thousands. We collected handfuls of them in baby food jars at recess and hid them in our open-front desks to play with during class!

At the kickball diamond, I was often chosen last by a reluctant team captain during P.E. I would chew my nails when I felt awkward, bouncing nervously against the chain-link fence behind me, where I waited... and waited.

Near there, on the other side of the fence, I had once picked up a scorched matchbook while walking with a friend. She had sniffed at it and said it had been used to light a joint. *Pakalolo,* or *Maui Gold,* as marijuana was called in the islands, was a prohibited drug smoked by rebellious kids. I never got near it.

The big multi-purpose building on the other side of the school entrance was used for many things. *Duh!* Every month, a new lunch menu revealed what the cafeteria was going to serve. We would pay 25¢ for a compartment tray of foods with a pint-sized carton of white milk, and then proceed to an assigned fold-out table on wheels.

When those tables were folded up halfway into the air and rolled to the side, we would use the room for assemblies, or the school play, or P.E. on a rainy day, or extra-curricular activities. This was the very dance floor on which I learned the Charleston

THE JOY WEAVER - GRASSROOTS

Shuffle in tap and jazz class after school. It is also where I debuted at my first and only school dance, before Christmas break of my sixth-grade year.

My parents' generation had been raised on the quip, "Don't drink, dance, smoke, or chew. And don't go out with guys (girls) who do." So, I had been cautiously allowed to attend the school dance after demonstrating my unprovocative side to side shuffle for Dad. He strictly forbade me from slow dancing. My parents' Bible-based standards were in place to protect me from the troubles that many of my classmates were already falling into.

One day, standing near the monkey bars at recess, my insides were churning. A couple classmates were circulating the playground with a poll, "Who's your favorite actor?" I felt like such a nerd sometimes! Most public-school kids knew all the latest and greatest Hollywood stars. Since my parents were choosy about what they allowed me to watch, I surely did not. I wanted to think of an answer before the kids got to me. It was nerve wracking.

The first people that popped into my mind were Tim Conway and Don Knots, from family-friendly Disney films. I thought they were hilarious; but was my choice too childish to some people? Should I offer my actual opinion, or name a more popular celebrity I'd heard about? I dreaded the thought of being laughed at.

When the surveyors came my way and repeated their inquiry, I took a deep breath and responded truthfully. I don't even remember their reactions because I was so happy to have answered authentically. As far as I was concerned, I had passed a big test! And I was pretty sure God was pleased with the results, too.

That same year God touched my heart with a desire to reach kids at school who did not know the Lord. I felt His love for them with deep intensity. I would cry on my pillow at night, asking God to show me ways to talk to them without being embarrassed. One person on my mind was my sweet Vietnamese friend, Minh.

Nancy McComb

I wanted her to know Jesus - The Way, The Truth, and The Life (**John 14:6**) - so she could go to heaven one day.

Our fifth-grade friendship had been growing throughout the year. Just before summer, we were chosen to serve together as attendants in the May Day Parade on campus. We strolled like Hawaiian princesses, wearing silky sky-blue gowns and leafy green headbands, strumming our ukuleles. It was so much fun!

I remember being especially bold at recess one time. We were sitting on a log at the edge of the playground, facing each other a few feet apart. I told her who Jesus was. He was God's Son, born of the Virgin Mary. He had lived a perfect life and then died on the cross to save her (and everyone!) from sin. He had risen from the dead and offered eternal life. He loved her and wanted to live inside of her heart.

Though she did not invite Him into her life that day, I continued to pray that she would ask Him to be her Savior later. I still do every time I think of her.

Romans 1:16a *"For I am not ashamed of the gospel, for it is the power of God for salvation to everyone who believes..."*

12 AWANA

A new girl named Debbie came during sixth grade. Her dad was a Marine and her family attended Kailua Baptist Church. Apart from meeting her in public school, I never would have known her. She invited me to a youth discipleship program called AWANA (Approved Workmen Are Not Ashamed). I joined her regularly on Tuesday nights for several semesters, even after we had both switched schools. The A-frame roof of Debbie's church looked like the first letter of AWANA!

AWANA is based on **2 Timothy 2:15** *"Be diligent to present yourself approved to God as a workman who does not need to be ashamed, accurately handling the word of truth."* Their website states, "With an unwavering commitment to the gospel, AWANA is being used to reach over 4 million kids every week in 120 countries, giving children and youth from every background an opportunity to know, love and serve Jesus for a lifetime." (awana.org, 12/9/21)

This was a Christian kids' club par excellence! Thoroughly trained AWANA leaders in spiffy uniforms led the competitive games between four teams: Red, Green, Yellow and Blue. Each team would gather along their colored line of the huge AWANA game square taped to the floor. After an explanation of the game at hand, one member of each team would crouch at the team's starting pin, ready for the whistle blast. "Brrrrreeeeet!" Then they were off and competing for points!

We might be throwing bean bags at a line of pins, or tugging rope against a team across the circle, or balancing circle pins on our heads while walking, or passing batons in a relay. The roof and walls of the church gym would vibrate with the echoes of rubber soles squeaking and the shouts of eager kids cheering on their teammates. Once a player had completed the course, he or she would make a mad dash for the middle to acquire the first-place pin or the second-place beanbag! And the scorekeeper was always keeping track.

At Handbook Time each small group, by age and gender, would head to their classroom with a leader to talk and pray, welcome visitors, and "say sections." Sections were 1-2 pages with a simply-stated Bible doctrine and supporting verses. These illustrated lessons were spiralbound in a book in logical succession. We earned AWANA "script" for each section we had memorized and could recite aloud. The yellow paper money allowed us to buy things in the AWANA store. We also earned patches and pins to attach to our uniforms as we progressed.

We had energetic fun and learned the Word of God at the same time. I wrote about AWANA in my diary many times during the last semester I attended.

<u>Jan 5, 1982</u> We played lots of fun games. First, we went around the circle once with a paper bag on our heads to try and get the pin or the beanbag. I got the pin (10 points). Said 7 sections and got to keep my braid. I'm saving for a neclece which is 40 scrip. I have 20 more to go. There are 29 left in my book. Bye-Bye.

<u>Jan 26, 1982</u> Awana was really fun. I was Debbie's twin.

THE JOY WEAVER - GRASSROOTS

<u>Mar 2, 1982</u> ...mom came and we had to go to AWANA tonight. I had enough to get the necklace but it wasn't there tonight because they were only selling books. It was red, white, and blue night. And had hot dogs and stuff there for supper.

<u>Mar 9, 1982</u> Then I got ready for AWANA. It was zoo night and I dressed up as a fox. I said my two sections. If I bring a person next week, I'll finish my book and then I'll get my next book. I got the necklace. It's beautiful. It has a little anchor charm, a heart charm, and a cross. It cost 40 script but it was worth it.

<u>Mar 16, 1982</u> It was Mystery Box night at "<u>AWANA</u>". I got my new book but I still have to finish my last section in my other book.

   Debbie's invitation to AWANA provided me with my first overview of Biblical theology. For eighteen months I was being creatively motivated to hide hundreds of Bible passages in my heart. They helped me to know why I believed what I believed. They taught me how to think and act as a follower of Jesus. The Holy Spirit would bring these truths to mind over weeks, months, and years as I would continue to grow in my faith, unashamed. (Mind you, I did *not* say untempted.)

2 Timothy 3:16-17 *"All Scripture is inspired by God and profitable for teaching, for reproof, for correction, for training in righteousness; so that the man of God may be adequate, equipped for every good work."*

13 A WHALE OF A TALE

Sixth grade booster class at Aikahi Elementary was for highly motivated achievers. The creative hands-on class exposed us to varied learning opportunities, like the time we journeyed to the neighboring island of Maui to do some whale watching. We prepared for the unique field trip by doing research, and I made another book.

Each year in November, an estimated 10,000 humpback whales migrate from the harsh winter waters of Alaska to the warm tropical waters of the Hawaiian Islands. They leave the diminishing food sources up north to begin breeding season in the south until around May. Other groups of humpback whales migrate north to south similarly, all around the globe. However, the Hawaiian Islands support the only National Marine Sanctuary for humpback whales in the world.[11]

Humpback whales weigh 80,000 – 90,000 pounds as adults. These massive creatures seem to be showing off with their unique maneuvers. Breaching is when they torpedo through the surface and plumet back down in clouds of ocean spray. If they gently "peek" headfirst above the surface, it is called a spy hop. They can be seen "waving" their fluke (tail) or slapping their pectoral fins on the water, as if to greet their fans. Fountains of ocean water shoot out of their blowholes when they respirate.[12] I was excited! Soon our class would be watching them for real!

THE JOY WEAVER - GRASSROOTS

Public school staff chaperoned our select group of students across the island waters for several days and nights. We drove to the airport for our flight out, took off and landed, stayed in a hotel, went shopping and ate our meals in the coastal town of Lahaina. But the best part would be watching the entertaining whales from our tour boat! I couldn't wait to see, hear, taste, touch and smell all that we had imagined! How many whales would we see? Would we get to see some babies, too?

When the big day came, we bounced across the ocean bay through the breezy salt air in a glass-bottomed boat. Propelling toward the open blue ocean, we had an unhindered view into the depths beneath us. That did freak me out! I imagined any number of threats cracking the glass between us and the waters we were riding!

We looked and looked for signs of whales near the surface, or even underneath us. No matter where we looked, we could not find them. Sadly, that day in the spring of 1981, we were sorely disappointed with failure. Regardless of the ample preparations made by us and our school staff, the time and money that had been spent, and the beautiful blue-sky weather, not a single whale breached, spy hopped, pec slapped, waved a fluke in the air, or even bothered to appear for us in any way!

Although we had observed some dolphins, the big letdown clouded my thoughts after that trip for years. Thinking back now, I recollect dinner at twilight on the patio of an open-air restaurant by the beach. I see us wandering between packed shelves of splashy trinkets in the tourist-trap shops. Racks of swirly turquoise mother-of-pearl necklaces, pink puka shell earrings, and green jade bracelets caught our fancy. Ceramic figurines of

Hawaiian girls danced hula on the shelves and ceramic bouquets of plumeria looked good enough to smell. A lavish purchase would be the white ceramic whale on a gnarly piece of driftwood or a bright oil painting of island life. I bought an airbrushed graphic-T or cellophaned box of chocolate macadamia nuts. There were plumeria scented soaps, gardenia scented candles, bottles of beach sand, and so much more! How could I have forgotten?

But there was one unforgettable souvenir rubbing my conscience raw: the regret of having surrendered to temptation in the airport before our flight. A teacher traveling with our co-ed group must have thought she was doing us girls a favor by reading aloud an explicit teen romance as we waited at the gate. Impregnating words trickled over the pages like a magic love potion spilling from a forbidden room. The intimate details would be hard to forget. My insides were tingling, taunting.

I had not received an update on puberty or romance since Mom had read to my brother and I in first and second grades from the Christian book *Fearfully and Wonderfully Made!* Now, sitting at the teacher's feet in that circle of girls, I was suffering with frustrating longings. Wisdom in my conscience had warned me, even cried out to me, not to listen to the story of teenage fornication. I had battled with lust and lost, refusing that first strong inclination to walk away. I felt dirty. I was disappointed in myself. What was the point of daydreaming about such things while I was still a kid? It would be years until I could fall in love and get married.

A few months later, the Holy Spirit began working on my soul about wrong things I had done and kept hidden. I wrote in my journal, "I would think of the bad things I had done and feel guilty whenever the subject of Christianity came up."

THE JOY WEAVER - GRASSROOTS

My heart and mind could bear it no longer after a convicting message from Pastor Jim one Sunday evening. I just had to tell Mom something when she came to kiss me goodnight. "I confessed dumping my school lunches for years, and not brushing my teeth when I said I had." These confessions would take a few weeks; one or two at a time, at first...

"One night I said some simple sin and Mom forgave me, as usual. As she left, she patted my feet and said, "Now you're clean as a green bean." Silly. But it began to trigger in my brain the biggest mess of unconfessed sins I'd not realized had grown so large. I tried to shove them out of my mind, but I couldn't sleep. I felt terrified that I'd have to confess all those things, but my mind left me no other choice.

I was crying and miserable, so I grabbed my white blanket for support, went downstairs timidly and just stood in front of my parents, who were watching T.V., and cried. Mom couldn't figure out what was wrong and finally asked if I wanted to talk about something. I said yes and climbed even more miserably back upstairs to bed waiting for Mom. And in the end Dad came along there, too."

I confessed I had graffitied a tree in the middle of our townhouse complex by carving my name in it. I was now aware I had vandalized private property. I had watched a dirty TV show with my friend at a sixth-grade house party. And who knows what else I divulged. Then came time to release the tawdry trip tale. Ugh!

It was embarrassing to be so vulnerable with my mom and dad. But each fresh start had been worth the cost of full disclosure. So, on I went. They listened kindly as I told my story and said how sorry I was for not having left the group before the book got racy. After some fact-finding questions, they forgave me again. I was a dandelion puff on the summer breeze…and exhausted. I needed to get some sleep! We all said good-night again and they headed back downstairs. I closed my eyes.

But soon, one last group of memories bubbled up from shadowy depths like sticky molten lava. I shuddered. They were from a long time ago when we had been living in Honduras. *SIGH*. Mom and Dad were already watching their show again. We were all weary from unexpected emotional conversations… It was late… I had already been so brave… Couldn't I deal with this stuff some other time?

The firm but gentle invitation of the Holy Spirit was not going away. As I lay in the stillness of my cozy room, I pondered the possible outcome of moving forward. I wanted to resist God, but I also imagined complete relief. I gathered courage to call my parents back. "I spilled my guts like I never had before and never wanted to again.

I'm not sure how much better I felt at first. I knew I had had to do what I did, and I slept soundly afterwards. But I felt torn open and transparent and weird. That's the only way I can describe it. I wondered what things would be like with Mom and Dad knowing now. I wanted desperately to just forget the whole thing.

I don't think that's something everyone does, and I don't think everyone feels guilt as much as I do. Though I felt weird and awkward revealing all my hidden sins, I think I would be different now if I had not. It set me free – opened the way for honesty and trust and communication in my relationship to my parents.

This was not the end of giving in to temptations or needing to confess and repent. We are always at war with the flesh as we learn to walk by the Holy Spirit (**Galatians 5:16-17**). But thanks to my pastor and my parents, I was learning how the Holy Spirit of Jesus could wash me clean with the truths of His Word (**John 15:3**) and the renewing power of His shed blood (**Titus 3:5-7**). God was training me how to break sin's grip on me and how to be an overcomer (**1 Corinthians 15:55-57**). God's power had broken new ground in me for spiritual growth. I loved Him so much more!

Psalm 51:1-3 *"Be gracious to me, O God, according to Your lovingkindness; According to the greatness of Your compassion blot out my transgressions. Wash me thoroughly from my iniquity, And cleanse me from my sin. For I know my transgressions, And my sin is ever before me."*

1 John 1:9 *"If we confess our sins, He is faithful and righteous to forgive us our sins and to cleanse us from all unrighteousness."*

Psalm 103:1-5 *"Bless the Lord, O my soul, And all that is within me, bless His holy name. Bless the Lord, O my soul, And forget none of His benefits; Who pardons all your iniquities, Who heals all your diseases; Who redeems your life from the pit, Who crowns you with lovingkindness and compassion; Who satisfies your years with good things, So that your youth is renewed like the eagle."*

14 BEAUTIFUL MUSIC

Mom and Dad loved music and bathed us in it from the time we were babies. Dad had built that beautiful stereo cabinet for my mom, so we could all enjoy listening to records and cassettes. Mom sang with me around the house, *"Jesus loves the little children…"* or *"I had a little chickee…"* or *"Just a closer walk with Thee…"* or *"I know a wiener man…"* And sometimes we sang phrases back and forth for fun. When Dad showed me how to whistle in the carport, I puckered my lips and spit air through them again and again without success. Finally, I figured out how to gently project my breath through the tight squeeze and turn out a tune.

After we moved to Hawaii, my parents were able to buy a used piano! Mom had played as a kid, and Dad had played a trombone in one of his school bands. He still had it! The brown hard-shell case with red velvet lining cradled two long pieces of brass: the bell tube with bell and the slide tube with mouthpiece. Dad's repertoire had been left behind, but we delighted when he connected the long parts together and slid the tube back and forth, blasting a few deep notes. MomMom, Dad's mom, played piano and organ as a missionary and pastor's wife. Grandma, Mom's mom, had played the piano every night for her family. There was plenty of music appreciation and musical talent to be passed on from our relatives.

Mom and Dad provided three years of piano lessons for me during middle school. Influenced by the strict discipline of an accomplished performance teacher and the tick-tock of a metronome, I thrived. "Persistent Practice Produces Proficient Pianists," she said. I plunked each note tediously at the start, fingers raised above the keys, first with the right hand and then with the left. I was instructed to do this 10x each hand separately, and then play the piece at least 10 more times, bringing the treble clef and bass clef together. I did my best to be patient with the process.

Eventually, I would be able to concentrate on the mood and flow, until my rendition sounded something like my teacher's masterful performance. An unusual friend became my audience during piano practice, too often to be a coincidence. Charlie the gecko would appear from behind a ceiling beam in the family room and venture part way down the wall to join me. Secured to the wood paneling by the tiny suction cups on his "sticky" feet, he would chirp along with the music.

Our church family at International Baptist loved to worship the Lord in song. The congregation would unify in harmonious praise through the measures of soprano, alto, tenor, and bass notes in the hymnbook. Special numbers by the choir in the loft was something to which I looked forward. And every Sunday, we heard a soloist, vocal ensemble, or instrumentalist who directed our focus on God. On occasion, we hosted special performers like The Bowker Brothers. I was ecstatic, watching them play complex duets on one or both pianos, positioned sideways to display their fingers dancing on the keys. I sure did buy one of their records!

As our family drove place to place around the island, I would sing in the car a lot. Sometimes this made my brother crazy. But if Dad was playing a Sixteen Singing Men cassette, I could not resist joining the euphoric synergy of masculine voices in a quadruple quartet. Or if one of Amy Grant's new releases played on 95.5

KAIM FM, my soul could not stay silent. I would sing into the sidewall of our Ford Pinto, riding the tones and rhythms of her voice as if it was my own.

Her lyrics seemed to come right out of my heart. I totally got her! Or she got me. She was just a down-to-earth, Jesus-lovin' girl. I knew this because I had seen and heard her at one of her earliest ever concerts. KAIM radio had helped host her at the Blaisdell Arena, and my dad had performed her sound check. She was a casual teenager that night, sittin' on a stool in blue jeans and white t-shirt. She had "talked story" about her life, strummed her guitar, and sang her songs. No band. Just Amy.

Her music fueled my faith for years! She sang authentically *Beautiful Music*. I was challenged by songs like *Old Man's Rubble* and *Fat Baby*, or tickled with *Grape, Grape Joy*. I echoed her prayer to have *My Father's Eyes* and celebrated with her on the *Mountain Top*. God used her to give me *A New Song* that voiced my prayers and praises to *El Shaddai*. I have been reminded ever since those days of *Angels Watching Over Me*, and I determined like her to walk *Straight Ahead* with Jesus.

Someone at church thought it would be a fun idea to form a youth choir. So, on November 9, 1980, my journal states, "**our choir sung in Evening Service for the first time. We will be called The International Victory Singers. It was a pretty good performance. We sang** *Happiness* and *I Have Decided to Follow Jesus*."

My friend and I were invited to sing a duet one Sunday night. We sang along with my ukulele and practiced many times. We were nervous about being up in front of everyone! Dad had offered wise advice. "Keep your focus on Jesus. You are singing for Him." Erin and I sang on stage with shaky voices, *I Wish We'd All Been Ready*. Nerves were smothering our vocal cords. I prayed silently that God would use the song to help the congregation reflect on being ready for Jesus' return.

Church was a place I felt safe and loved, surrounded by a body of believers who were almost all friends like family. I believed in the things we sang about – God's melody of love, His forgiveness of our sins, His joy as strength, His provision in need, His comfort for sorrow, His power of creation, His friendship in prayer, His desire for the lost. I was glad to be in the house of the Lord and to worship Him.

I also loved most music in general. We had grown up listening to many kinds of compositions at home – juvenile, classical, popular, included. But recently Dad had set a family precedent that we stick to Christian music. I hit middle school and high school in the eighties. So you know what that means: artists like The Police, Queen, Talking Heads, Foreigner, U2, and Abba; or Lionel Richie, Prince, Boy George, Cindy Lauper, Tina Turner, and Michael Jackson. Whitney Houston was outrageously amazing! The Eagles and Chicago; or Kenny Rogers and Dolly Parton; Eddie Rabbit, Juice Newton, The Judds, and on and on and on. The secular artists from my day would hold America's fancy, and mine, for a long, long time.

While I understood my dad's choice in principle, I had not yet grown to discern the fact that we become what we behold. My emotions were like guitar strings being plucked by the tunes of any powerful melody, joyful or jaded, sacred and secular. Everybody I knew liked both. It didn't seem to matter all that much. The tug-of-war between godly and worldly affections would leave me conflicted for many years. And I know I wasn't alone in that. I have a distinct memory of hanging out with youth group friends in the church parking lot by our cars one night. One of them was playing music from the car stereo, *Burning Down the House* by Talking Heads. My double-minded, divided loyalty was going to be difficult to manage.

Psalm 33:1-3 *"Sing for joy in the Lord, O you righteous ones; Praise is becoming to the upright. Give thanks to the Lord with the lyre; Sing praises to Him with a harp of ten strings. Sing to Him a new song; Play skillfully with a shout of joy."*

1 John 2:15-16 *"Do not love the world nor the things in the world. If anyone loves the world, the love of the Father is not in him. For all that is in the world, the lust of the flesh and the lust of the eyes and the boastful pride of life, is not from the Father, but is from the world."*

15 A WISE MOVE

Ten years into marriage, shortly after moving to Hawaii, Mom and Dad squeezed every dollar from savings to buy their first home. The 2-story, 3 bed/3 bath townhome was sandwiched between townhouses just like it. We lived twenty minutes from church, thirty-five minutes from KAIM radio station, and a few miles from Aikahi Elementary School. This *windward* northeast side of the island was quieter than the *leeward* southern side, harboring Honolulu and Waikiki. Housing was less expensive, while still being nestled amid grocery stores, gas stations, shopping centers, banks, post offices, restaurants, bowling alleys, movie theaters and more.

Neighborly clusters of dwellings were in juxtaposed rows of townhomes. Front-door courtyards exited to sidewalks along the asphalt parking spaces. Rear views overlooked steep hills dressed in thick green leaves with yellow flowers, or grassy fields, or fun playgrounds. Our living room sliding-glass doors opened onto flat green grass around a playground of climbing logs, tire swing, merry-go-round, and a slide. Our dining room picture window framed a giant shade tree off to the right.

We had so many friends! My neighbor Lexi and I created a kids' club. John, Chad, Anna, Esther, Jason, Fiona, and others traded marbles, played hopscotch, climbed trees, rode bikes, roller skated, swung on the tire swing, climbed the logs, spun on the merry-go-round, and made snow cones with my Snoopy shaved ice machine. A huge green lawn at the base of a nearby hill was where we played kickball or tag. There were very few rules to worry about in this kid-friendly development.

The community pool was available every day for swimming and could be signed out for activities like family potlucks. The city bus stop was next to the main entrance of the whole private property. For 25₵ we could go anywhere on the island by hopping on a safe and clean city bus. A transfer ticket was free if connections were necessary. Most of us kids used the city bus to get to and from public school.

As I neared the age of middle school, Mom and Dad began praying about where to send me. John would have to come too. Most upper-level public schools had poor reputations of low education standards and drug problems. St. Mark Lutheran was a small Christian school on our side of the island. But how could my parents afford tuition? God provided through KAIM radio station! Dad was on loan to them from our mission, so KAIM had not had to pay him a salary. They decided to contribute by helping with children's education funds. So off to St. Mark's we went!

Our townhouse neighborhood continued to be busy and friendly. My first paid jobs were babysitting neighbors' kids, for 25₵ an hour. Grandparents and a great grandma visited us at separate times. Great Grandma housesat in a townhome for a month! As the years went by, friends in the neighborhood moved away. John and I grew closer to church and school kids, and we would invite them to come hang out.

We both had friends sleeping over when the infamous Hurricane Iwa slammed into us in the black of night. Shingles blew off our roof! Rain drenched the attic via 22 leaks we tried to catch in buckets! The storm knocked out our electricity, too. Us kids played cards by candlelight after trying to help Mom inside. Outside, Dad had to put our leaky roof repair on hold when KAIM radio station went off the air. He was the engineer in charge of restoring the broadcast; so off he went to the other side of Oahu!

My parents loved having friends over, too. Guests around our dinner table could be missionaries or colleagues, college kids from church, or friends young and old to celebrate one of our birthdays. One time, Mom hosted a group of church ladies for a sleep over. As I was heading upstairs from the older crowd to make myself scarce, something shot past me and hit the wall I was climbing beside. Mom had launched a pair of Dad's tighty-whities like a giant rubber band! It slid down and draped itself on the stairway light while all the ladies were cackling wildly! Mom was fun.

…KAIM's tuition contribution lasted for two years until Dad's service for them became only part-time. He had begun teaching and administrating at International Baptist Bible College, associated with our church. Though Mom was contributing most of her earnings to our tuition as well, those funds would no longer be enough without the extra help.

So, Mom and Dad had big decisions to make once again. Where would John and I go to high school? St. Mark's Lutheran was only K-8. And how would they get us there? Most private Christian high schools were on the other side of the island. In addition, private high school tuition costs would be more expensive; so how would they pay for them? Finances were already tight, with other facets of their budget being challenged as well. They took their time praying about it and asked close friends for the "wisdom of many counselors." The answer eventually came.

They would sell our townhouse and use part of the equity to help pay for school. Our new problem would be where to live? Homes closer to work and a new school on the other side of the island were expensive! My Dad learned it would be more cost-effective in the short-term and long-term to build a house. God led my parents to a rocky hillside property, near close friends, at just the right price! However, it would take over a year to excavate, prepare blueprints, buy materials, pour a foundation, pay just a few contractors, get some help from qualified friends, and D.I.Y. the finishing work ourselves, day by day, for months.

As I graduated from eighth grade, we sold our happy home of six years, packed up our stuff, and stored it all at Camp Timberline. Since we were due for a summer home assignment on the mainland, we could figure out later where to live when we returned. And sure, I was excited about road-tripping again, but attending a new school in the fall was a worrisome prospect. I wouldn't know anyone there! All too soon, my next chapter in life was going to be "High School and Homeless."

16 ON EAGLES' WINGS

Finishing junior high at St. Mark Lutheran meant huge transitions were ahead. I had been there for two years and enjoyed myself immensely. Chapel services in a Lutheran school had given me different perspectives of Christian faith. Clergy members wore crispy black dress shirts, the black collar folded over a stiff white collar, with only a square of white peeking out between the neck buttons. Altar boys carried golden rods with bell-shaped snuffers to smother candles after service. Pews had hinged boards at floor-level, on which to kneel while Father so-in-so wiped ash on our foreheads. I absorbed a different kind of formal church conduct.

School had been enlightening, and I worked hard to get good grades. The science teacher taught us that cockroaches clean themselves like cats do, meticulously. The PE teacher motivated me to exercise my pudgy adolescent body. I needed that push! The choir director taught us a lively band tune called *76 Trombones*. I always felt like I was marching in that *"big parade"* when we sang! My art teacher taught us to sketch a self-portrait with super scientific symmetry.

And small class sizes meant big fun! Twenty-eight of us stuck together through every subject. My buddy Robby called me "Sister Nancy - shipped in a box from India" after a local palm reader by the same name. Classmate Josh was so gullible! If we gave him a lead line like "Did you see her, that one girl?" he would bust out with a story that cracked us up. We had nobody real in mind, but he sure did! He must have liked the attention. Somebody in our class put their bottom-print on a window louver when no one else was looking – hopefully! The jalousie had been dusty quite a while. The discovery of the tell-tale outline was shocking and amusing when we all returned to class!

I spent countless sleepovers at Tina's. We loved eating snacks while playing *Brian's Song* on the piano, singing *Blue Moon,* and trying to moonwalk like Michael Jackson in his music video, *Thriller*. We would swim in her pool, talk about belly fat, try on makeup, invent silly songs like *The Frito Bandito*, and giggle ourselves to sleep. And her mom prepared the only fish I ever ate happily. It was oven-baked with butter and Mediterranean herbs!

Moving on to high school apart from Robby and Tina and others would be the worst good-bye since leaving my friends in Honduras. Many classmates would attend Redeemer Lutheran High School in downtown Honolulu. But I would be at Hawaii Baptist Academy in Nuuanu because it was five minutes away from where my parents worked then, at the Bible college at our church.

Since Mom and Dad had decided to sell our townhome, partly to pay for mine and John's schooling, and since we did not know where all we would live throughout the building process, years of stabilizing factors were being dismantled. And if that wasn't enough transition, we would soon head to the mainland for an eight-week road trip across the U.S. It had been three years since we had visited relatives, friends, and churches.

Most of those weeks on the road are a blur to me now. Living out of a suitcase, place to place, clothed me with insecurity. Losing my middle school friends and missing a lot of summer fun with my church friends made me feel lonely. Having no place to call

THE JOY WEAVER - GRASSROOTS

home anymore, I was listless. And the idea of going to a new school with complete strangers left my mind to stare at blank faces. As a moody teenager, I was continually challenging Mom, Dad, and John with my bad attitudes.

One evening, we came to Mom's brother's house. We were glad to pile in for a rare visit and surround Uncle Eric with our love. He had been plagued with addictions ever since I had known him. Growing up, his parents had moved him just before his senior year. His older sisters had already graduated. In the wake of deeply rooted friendships at church and school being ripped away, he became rebellious and never resolved his trauma.

He loved us a lot and was always hospitable. But I'm not sure how glad he was to have *me* visit that time! When I was told to go to bed at 9PM, I complained! The Michigan sun was glowing hot on the horizon through the downstairs window. How could I go to bed in broad daylight?! I cried myself to eventual sleep in miserable frustration. I was sick of feeling like I had no control and nothing to hold on to!

Days later, we arrived at Dad's sister's place in upstate New York. Aunt Lorraine and Uncle Chuck were so much fun! Uncle Chuck would tease and talk non-stop or play his accordion jubilantly. Aunt Lorraine would cook mounds of savory dishes, including recipes from her MK days in Puerto Rico. She collected Drost tins in the kitchen and all sizes and shapes of wall mirrors hung throughout the house. Their entertaining Jesus-loving family was filled out by my cousins: Joy, Nate, and Heidi. They were a bit younger than me and John.

With suitcases in hand, we had come ready to catch up from three years of lost time in just a day or two. I talked excitedly as some of us ladies had entered the kitchen together. Mom and I pulled out small bags of fresh purple cherries purchased at roadside stands along the way: first $1.00/lb., then $.50/lb., then $.25/lb! We had not been able to resist the deals getting better and better. So we had brought a LOT of cherries!

Cousin Joy had been a kindred spirit since the early years. It's like my heart would beat faster any time we got together. As little girls, we had practiced the hymn *This is My Father's World* to sing as a duet for our families. Setting up rows of chairs downstairs to give a little concert, we had called everyone to come and listen. We sang every verse and chorus. That song became a lifelong favorite for me, if not for them.

We were older now, and I was also enjoying a budding friendship with Heidi. When it came time to go to sleep, us girls were arranged on makeshift beds in the attic so all nine of us would fit in the townhouse. Lying on my back, soft conversations wound down until only dark silence hovered between myself and the heat-retaining rafters. Joy and Heidi, now asleep nearby, were a comfort. But the restlessness inside of me was keeping me awake.

Silent prayers toward heaven brought warm silky tears rolling down my cheeks. I wondered what was wrong with me lately and what to do with myself. I was weary. In the quiet, a clear narrative ran through my mind. *"...those who wait for the Lord will gain new strength; They will mount up with wings like eagles. They will run and not get tired, They will walk and not grow faint."* I was surprised! Had I ever memorized those verses? God's presence was nearly tangible, and I drifted off to sleep pondering those words.

In the morning, as I came into the bathroom where my mom was doing her hair and makeup, she gave me a word of encouragement. "I don't know all that's going on with you, Nance, so I've been asking the Lord how best to help. I'm not really sure, but

He did give me this verse for you." And can you guess which verse she quoted? *"...those who wait for the Lord will gain new strength..."* **Isaiah 40:31**.

I was startled. It felt like a miracle! Out of all the thousands of verses in the Bible, she was giving me the very same one that God had given me the night before. Nothing of this magnitude had ever happened to me before! I knew again in that moment how close God was. There was no doubt in my mind that He loved me and was communicating with me personally. It was special between Mom and I, too, since I realized she was hurting with me.

When I began my freshman year at Hawaii Baptist Academy (HBA) that fall, I encountered another surprise. Our school mascot was the eagle, and our theme verse was **Isaiah 40:31**! My God, Immanuel, was demonstrating His manifest presence. How reassuring! He was teaching me to lean on Him as I headed into the unknown, and I was certain He was right there with me!

Psalm 139:1-6 *"Oh Lord, You have searched me and known me. You know when I sit down and when I rise up; You understand my thought from afar. You scrutinize my path and my lying down, and are intimately acquainted with all my ways. Even before there is a word on my tongue, Behold, O Lord, You know it all. You have enclosed me behind and before, And laid Your hand upon me. Such knowledge is too wonderful for me; It is too high, I cannot attain to it."*

17 DEDICATED

Sitting on a bench in the bleachers of the gym, my pulse began to quicken. I was midway up in the crowd of high school peers at Hawaii Baptist Academy in our expansive multipurpose facility. This was my first Spiritual Emphasis Week (SEW) at my new school, and the guest speaker had been inviting us to walk more faithfully with God. As he relayed messages from the Bible and shared his heart each day, I couldn't help but think about what he was saying. Yet was I ready to respond?

This second semester of freshman year, I was finally making friends in a class three times the size I had been used to. "Cool" is not a label anyone would have readily assigned to me. Maybe "nerd" or "goody-two-shoes." I loved Jesus, but "hypocrite" might have been a better term.

The year before, as middle school was ending at St. Mark Lutheran, I had gone to our eighth-grade graduation party feeling excited. My best friend, Tina, had done a makeover on me with an olive-colored T-shirt dress, a thin red belt, a big '80's hairdo, and extravagant makeup. We had even done a photo shoot beforehand! I felt a bit fat and conspicuous, but mostly grown-up pretty, instead of my usual little-girl cute.

The party turned out to be anything but cute. I had spent the night at Tina's house so my parents wouldn't know I was going. I definitely ran over that red flag! Our small class was a nice enough group of kids, but unattended adolescence exposed me to scenes I had never even imagined. I saw and did shameful things, and my normally good reputation was ridiculed by one of the boys. That hurt! I had confessed every known sin to my parents in 6th grade, but I had determined to keep that foolishness to myself.

A year later, I have no recollection who was sitting near me on the bleachers in SEW that day. What I clearly remember is God tugging on me with a familiar sense of conviction. The SEW speaker had asked us to consider an intelligent question. Would we take God for granted and use our salvation as a fire escape? Or would I commit my life to Jesus, and live wholly for His will, since He had shed His blood on the cross to buy my freedom?

At this point, the speaker called on us to decide. He was inviting us to come down front if we wanted to commit our lives to the Lord. There were so many people! By now my heart was pounding into my ribs, and my palms were sweaty. I wrestled internally for an awkward moment and then stood up. Trying not to trip or clunk too loudly down many aluminum stairs, I finally arrived on the glossy gym floor. The speaker prayed over us, but I was praying on my own deep inside. "God, I'll go anywhere you want me to go and do anything you want me to do. I'm yours."

I knew that I meant it wholeheartedly, but I wasn't sure what it meant! With curious anticipation, I tried to imagine what the future might hold. All I could "see" in my mind were endless white clouds. I had signed a blank check of surrender and given it to God for the rest of my life. Only time would tell what His plans were. But I was glad I had responded to His invitation.

18 PRAISE AND DEDICATION

I thank you, Lord, for happy years.
You've been with me all my life!
When I cried you dried my tears,
gave me peace about every strife.

I haven't always listened to
Your quiet, guiding voice.
And many times, as a consequence,
I've made a bad choice.

But Lord, you never laughed at me,
or said, "I told you so."
Instead, you said, "I love you,"
and kept helping me to grow.

Through all these years I haven't
shared my faith with all I should.
But now I give my life to you.
Please use it as you would.

Whatever you have planned for me
in the years that yet remain,
I'll follow you with willful heart
that precious souls be gained.

Though the changes won't be overnight,
you'll always be there to remind,
I must listen to your guiding voice
so that your perfect will I find.

© *March 7, 1984 Nancy*

19 BE ANXIOUS FOR NOTHING

The wrinkles of the bedspread bunched beneath me were like the ripples of my stomach twisting in me, very uncomfortable. The thought of starting school tomorrow, without my buddy Jenna, made me sick. Who would I hang out with now? I cried during my devotions, a.k.a. my personal quiet time with God.

Last year, after dedicating my life to Christ, I had begun to read the Bible regularly on my own. The Bible was packed with good advice and walking closer to Jesus had been helpful. But recently, I had begun to lose sight of my commitment to the Lord.

Sometimes, I would write long lists of prayer requests for friends, family, and neighbors. But maybe lately, my friends at church had put me on their prayer request lists! Tonight, I was feeling horribly nervous and alone. Jenna would not be attending HBA this semester. So, I pleaded with God to help me.

Tenth grade had been a blast all fall with my new best friend Jenna. She was a year older than me and already had her driver's license. I had met her at church youth group the last summer and discovered she lived close to where our new house was in Hawaii Kai! After we had finally moved in, Jenna and I had started hanging out. I was over the moon when I found out she would also attend Hawaii Baptist Academy! I would be able to ride with her sometimes, instead of with my parents and my brother.

Since Jenna and I attended church youth group and Christian school together, it was natural that we talked about God. We even witnessed to a guy at youth group who came from a broken home. We were counseling him against using alcohol to numb his pain. We also listened to and prayed with a girl at church who ended up running away after accusing her dad of physical abuse. We believed God was an important part of our lives…sometimes.

Jenna's adventures were on the wild side for me, which was thrilling. We weren't doing anything too bad. I liked to spend the night at her house. We would play games with her mom and little sister, drive around, go to the beach, or visit her old friend group.

Once we snuck out to cruise the highway along the coast under starry skies. Another time we visited her old guy friends at a party. I took my first sips of alcohol that night: Kahlua in milk and beer. I waited outside while she made out with a guy in his room, too. I tried to comfort her later when she mourned his callous use of her. Another time we talked about getting out of bed to smoke cigarettes. "Nah!" I said. That did not and never would appeal to me. I enjoyed that I was free to make my own decisions with her.

Bit by bit I began to face the consequences of my actions. The guy at youth group that we had been witnessing to heard about me trying alcohol at the party. He was mad. He called me on our old-fashioned corded phone and demanded, "How can you tell me to give my problems to God instead of drink, and then go have a beer?" He called me a hypocrite and said he didn't want to talk to me anymore. I tried to explain that I had only tasted it. It made no difference, and he shut me out for the most part.

I created friction at home because fun with Jenna had grown more important to me than respecting and honoring my parents.

THE JOY WEAVER - GRASSROOTS

I did not see how this grieved the Lord. I only cared about myself and what I wanted. My journal describes preference for Jenna's mom over my own. I completely missed the fact that it was easy to like her because she did not hold Jenna and me accountable for anything. My parents would not let go of me that easily.

One day, Jenna and I wanted to go to the beach so we could bronze ourselves in the Hawaiian sun. I needed permission from my parents. We left Jenna's house where I had slept over and went to my house. But my parents were not awake yet, since they had gotten home late the night before. So, we waited a while.

Nov 17, 1984 I cleaned the bathroom and Jenna cleaned my room for me. Then I went upstairs and woke up mom and dad and asked if I could go to the beach (very nicely). We went through the whole same thing about going somewhere safe. I argued for about ½ an hour. I tried so hard to be respectful and not lose my temper but ****! it's so hard! They wouldn't listen to anything I was saying without coming back with some argument against me.

Finally, dad said I could go but that he wasn't setting a pressident or anything. Mom was mad at dad for letting me go. I started back downstairs saying I'd ask Jenna how long we'd be gone. Dad yelled at me, "Get back here!!!" I said, "What?! I'm going to ask Jenna when we'll be back!" Then he told me to sit down on the sopha. We went back and forth for another five minutes and then I went and asked Jenna when we'd be back.

I told them we were going to the beach and then to her house and I'd be home about 4:00. Then they had to know exactly when I'd be leaving the beach and going to her house. I said about 2-4 hours. They wanted to know exactly when. I said I'd call when I got to Jenna's house and that STILL wasn't enough!!

"Well, what if it gets too late and you still haven't called?" they asked. I snapped, "Then obviously I'm still at the beach!" They said that wasn't enough. Finally, I walked out of the room saying I'd call at 12:00. Jenna said, "Common, you need to get out of here." And we left. She's such a sweetheart!

We finally arrived at a nearby beach park and set our towels on the sand to enjoy yellow sun and blue waters. We called my parents from her house to check in with them at noon as promised. Since they did not insist that I return home, we went back to the beach to darken our tans on a beautiful day. They let me stay with Jenna overnight again, probably weary from the fight.

Sadly, the remainder of that journal entry, my last one in 1984, continues to reveal my blatant disrespect and rebellious attitude toward my parents. I was following along with a girl who seemed to lack boundaries. Jenna could do whatever Jenna wanted. My discontent with the rules at my house was growing heated.

When I wanted to go to the beach on another occasion, my parents put their foot down with a firm "no." They explained their worry that two teenaged girls were targets for unsavory fellows. It was too risky. Dad told me that if I had a problem with his answer, I was welcome to ask God to change his mind.

I marched downstairs to my room and pleaded with the Lord! It was an interesting lesson on the role of the Holy Spirit. When nothing changed in my favor, at least from my vantage point, I screamed at the top of my lungs into my pillow, "I hate this place! I'm living in a prison!" Hot tears drenched my frustrated face.

Not long after, I received the news that Jenna had been in a car accident and had gone through her windshield. She was in recovery, and she was changing schools. I don't know what kept me from being able to visit her; but I do know that I didn't drive yet. Maybe both sets of parents were glad to have us separated?

Just like that, she was gone. I would be heading back to spring semester at Hawaii Baptist Academy without the best friend I had done everything with for six months. Now I had no idea what life would look like when lunch time came. What would I do? Where would I go? Who would I eat with?

My deep need had driven me straight back to the Lord. Laying there uncomfortably on my bed, sick with worry, I begged God to help me find new friends "tomorrow."

Then I opened my Bible to where I had lately begun reading and heeding again in Philippians. What came next amazed me!

Philippians 4:4-8 *"Rejoice in the Lord always; again I will say, rejoice! Let your gentle spirit be known to all men. The Lord is near. Be anxious for nothing, but in everything by prayer and supplication with thanksgiving let your requests be made known to God. And the peace of God, which surpasses all comprehension, will guard your hearts and your minds in Christ Jesus."*

Receiving **Isaiah 40:31** had been similar. But this time, God's manifest presence was more immediate and intense. He was holding my heart and instructing my mind. I was giddy with revelation, and I obeyed: I rejoiced! I reveled in His nearness. I prayed with thanksgiving. He filled me with peace, and I went to sleep.

The next day, I began to wander campus at lunch time. As I passed the hillside where a stone picnic table rested up top, a group of kids called out to me, "Nancy, come and eat with us!" The Lord had kept His promise. And I had found new friends.

20 DISTRACTED

Run! Abner was hot on my tail. I loved the exhilaration of sprinting just out of reach with my hair flying in the wind, and then stopping somewhere safe to catch my breath and laugh. Abner chased a lot of girls. And I would chase a lot of boys. This was only kindergarten!

From church parking lot to church bookstore, I chased one boy for four years right up into middle school. We had held hands during a church couples' skate in fifth grade. Our families chose to cross paths in Michigan during separate vacations on the mainland that summer. He was sure cute and nice. I just had to ask my mom at bedtime one night if I would be allowed to "go with" him if he ever asked me. He never did.

My seventh-grade journal shouted a new name with the pining of a girl's musings: He loves me? He loves me not? It was "not." Later, an eighth-grade newcomer to church became my first official boyfriend. I lasted two weeks with him before I realized I felt dumb. The relationship was awkward – I hardly knew him. He had recruited a youth group friend at the arcade to ask me to "go with" him. I used a friend to say, "I'm done."

One afternoon that summer, I knocked knees and lost my breath while walking along the sidewalk at a cabin club on Little Traverse Bay. Mom and Dad were right there with me when we ran into the new boy with his people. He was tall and handsome with a big smile and bright eyes. As we stopped for friendly greetings, I blushed like the sunset, with a giggly gaze. Back "home" at Grandpa's and Grandma's cabin, scrutinizing myself in the mirror, I wondered, "Am I pretty enough?" I kept my eyes peeled for the sight of him again when we were out and about. Shucks, no luck. How that boy had gotten under my skin!

Oh, man. Back on Oahu, entering ninth grade, I was able to rub shoulders with so many! Each class had a variety of shapes and sizes, colors, and ages. There were wise ones, simple ones, smooth-faced and pimpled ones, baulkers, believers, players, and achievers. How would I pair up with only one? Finding him would be a lot of fun!

Stories of flirting, pranking, and talking with boys were regularly recorded in the pages of 1985, far more than I recollected before reading back. Girls around me were boy crazy, too; some getting as much affection as they could want. I cheered on their kissing and cavorting, but I was aiming for true love before I got a taste of that.

Our church family retreated regularly to Camp Timberline high above Kapolei. We worshiped with the breeze in the trees of Ironwood Chapel, ingested comfort foods at the outdoor dining porch, and opened our hearts to Bible passages while our pastors preached in the lodge. Side by side and circled 'round, we kids could think, pray, joke, encourage, cry, and confess. With loving mentors helping raise us, I loved Jesus. But it was hard to focus on faith in the face of manliness and muscles.

I knew God's Word to be true and useful. A Biblical worldview was the basis of all subjects taught at Hawaii Baptist Academy. It made sense to me! I joined Bible studies, Servant Group, and went to Sunday School and church. The Navigators discipleship class was on Sunday afternoons. Our youth group planned a Passion Play production, with a second performance at a church on Maui! Whenever I sang special numbers in church, I prayed to honor God. So, who did I love more? Jesus or the boys?

My first official dates happened in the summer after ninth grade. My parents' divorced friend at church had a son come visit from Florida. He joined our youth group and took a liking to me. Our two outings to Downtown Honolulu were classy rides in his dad's convertible. After the second event, he kissed me quick while we faced each other on my borrowed front porch (my family's new house was still being built). By the time school opened in the fall, he had already gone back to Florida.

Following those six mischievous months with Jenna, I became close to two of the guys in my new friend group. One really liked me; and one I desperately liked!

So, one April evening in tenth grade spring, I leaned into each of my parents as they came into my room to say good night. Dad came first. "I told him all about being depressed about not having a boyfriend and how I wanted one. He tried encouraging me and then couldn't think of anything else to say. He said, 'Good night. I love you. Have a good sleep.' Then he left.

Mom came in a little later. She gave me all this advice about (the boy I wanted) and said the girls in her youth group who sat around, even if they were nice and pretty- if they waited around, they didn't get asked out. She said I could have him over any time, and I should invite him to the Senior banquet at church or any youth group activity. I said I didn't know; I'd just try and get him to notice that I liked him."

My first date with that very guy at school was headline news for me and my friends. I had been swooning over him for months, and finally he had invited me to a movie! When I learned it would be just the two of us, I became a nervous wreck.

THE JOY WEAVER - GRASSROOTS

Lord, I'm so confused. I should be jumping for joy. I found out he likes me. Oh my gosh! I'm so excited. Now I'm nervous though. I can't believe we're really going out!

I'm scared though now that I've started thinking about everything like "Who's gonna pay?" "Will Mom and Dad be home when I get home?" "Are we gonna kiss, hold hands, or something?" "And if we hold hands, can I keep my hands from sweating?" They're sweating right now just writing all this.

And what will we talk about? Will he be nervous too? Oooooh! I have so many questions and worries. During geometry I sat by him as usual, but I felt weird, different. I've got a terrible knot in my stomach. Lord, I need you to give me 'God-confidence' and help me be myself and relax...Dating is such a scary thing.

I wish we could get rid of nervousness and jitters and just be ourselves around each other... I know how much I like him, but I don't know how much he likes me.

Anyway, Lord, you know the whole situation and how embarrassed and nervous I was on my 2 dates last summer. Please give me courage to be myself. Help him not to give up on me if I'm quiet. Help him find a good movie for us to see. This whole thing won't even happen if we don't find a movie that mom and dad say O.K. to.

Help me do what pleases you and please, somehow help me not to be nervous! I don't know if there's ever been anyone who wasn't nervous on their first date, but if it be your will – PLEASE find a way to help me feel relaxed. I want to make this thing work but I know I can't. I have to let you work it out. Thank you for listening.

Thank you that you already know exactly what's going to happen. I can trust in you. Nothing can separate me from you; nothing can happen to me that you don't allow. Thanks, Lord, for being my friend and listening to my problem. Help me trust you.

Love, Your daughter, Nancy

Nancy McComb

My parents were busy the night I went out, so I got ready at a girl friend's house. Leslie loaned me a pastel-striped sweater and helped do my makeup and hair. The doorbell rang, and she welcomed my date into the kitchen. I smiled sheepishly at him. When I ran back upstairs to get my purse, I accidentally knocked over a lamp with candle bulbs and glass covers!

I was extremely happy and still nervous. When he drove around trying to find a parking place, I was praying! I did not want him to feel stressed or embarrassed. After dinner, he drove us to see *The Gods Must Be Crazy*. The absurdities of the scenarios in that movie cracked us both up! At least we did not have car or dress troubles like the actors on the bush road in Africa. Since I was scared about our own parting scenario, I had already planned to avoid any physical contact. It would be safer to stay aloof than be rejected. I did tell him that I had had a really nice time.

When I heard his mom had given him $20 to take me out, it was a blow. Was anyone ever going to really like me? Other than someone's mom, I mean! The flirting at school continued a while, but he had not asked me out again. A month later, on a bowling fieldtrip, a "friend" let me know she had interviewed him about me at a social gathering. He had told her he did not like me anymore. I was crushed! I struggled to disguise the horrible hurt.

"That's O.K." I say cheerfully. Inside my innards are melting and tangling up – I get up 'cauz it's my turn to bowl. I concentrate, aim, – gutter. 7 times consecutively – gutter. I'm laughing but is that a happy laugh or a cover up? It must be a cover up because my throat is tight and my head spinning. How do I react? My last ball is a 9. That's a little better – at least part of me is still here.

In the van back to school my mind is wandering. Behind my eyelids, an almost uncontrollable amount of liquid is building up, pressuring to be let out. I CAN'T - I'M IN FRONT OF PEOPLE. I laugh here and there but then get very quiet. I pray, "Lord, help me to accept it. Help me to remember that you know who the right person is."

In survival mode during classes, I focused on my schoolwork and was tired a lot. I even fell asleep sometimes. I distanced myself and ignored him so I would stop thinking about him.

No one likes to find out someone they really care about doesn't like them. I would ask myself, "What's wrong with me?" "Am I ugly or fat or maybe I'm just boring or something." My self-confidence had been kind of crushed. But all the Bible reading and personal devotions is helping, because I know the Lord was with me and I had such a peace most of the day. I took his name stickers off my folders… scratched his name out in places. I didn't talk to him or smile at him or look at him as much.

Weeks later, school traded places with summer vacation. Youth group was a safe spot to bury sorrow in ice-cream sundaes, surf, and sand. June, July, and August became a blend of growing and groaning, in and among our fun-loving bunch of kids.

Some days I journaled Bible verses, notes, and prayer request lists for family and friends. The Holy Spirit was getting down to business with me again mid-summer when I wrote **"Things I need to repent of and turn over to the Lord."** Other days…

I longed for a boy to share life with. I was always watching, waiting, and wishing.

21 IN HIS TIME

(A prayer for my future husband)

Lord, sometimes I'm curious
and I begin to wonder,
Is he all right? Is he OK?
What happened in his life today?
Was it happy? Was it sad?
Was it good or maybe bad?

I wish that I could be there,
just standing by his side.
I wish that I could share his life,
his love, and joy and pride.

Or maybe he feels lost and hurt
and things aren't going right.
I wish I could encourage him,
pray with him, squeeze him tight.

Lord, you know I get impatient.
I just can't pretend I don't.
I fret and whine and huff and sigh
as many, many days go by,
and still it seems that as of yet,
my handsome prince I haven't met.

Handsome prince? I take that back.
I don't know what he's like.
He could be tall. He could be short.
He may like sports or like to hike.

THE JOY WEAVER - GRASSROOTS

His eyes could be blue, brown or green,
his reputation "norm" or "peachy keen."
His hair could be blonde, black, or brown.
He could be plain or the best in town.

Lord, I don't know what he's like.
All I can do is guess.
But thank you, Lord; I know your will
is that I have the best.

He's out there, Lord, I don't know where,
and 'til our paths you cross,
Dear Jesus, into your tender care,
I trust his precious life.

I pray he'll know and love you.
I pray your light he'll shine.
I pray you will protect us, '
til I am his and he is mine.
Please be with him through the valleys,
or when like an eagle, he soars high.
Through all the things that life will bring
help him grow, help him know
that always you'll be nigh.

And Lord, I give you my life.
Help me grow and learn your ways
so for him I'll be a good wife,
a helpmate all his days -
a source of close companionship,
in whom he can take pride -
a source of rest and comfort,
in whom he can confide.

Nancy McComb

To him I'll always listen
with empathy and care.
Whenever my love needs me,
I'll always be right there.

Together we will conquer
all the trials in our way,
as we commit our lives to you
each hour of every day.

We'll follow where you lead us,
wherever it might be.
We'll climb the highest mountain
or cross the widest, roughest sea.

Just saying that I love you, Lord,
is inadequate it seems,
but to show I really mean it,
I give you my goals, my hopes, my dreams.
Please nurture and develop them
any way that you see fit.

God, you sent your son to die for me
upon that wretched cross.
And you were willing on my account,
to suffer such great loss.

By this I know you love me,
so I place into your care
the life of my own precious one,
still unknown to me out there.

© *July 25, 1985 Nancy*

22 A FIRM FOUNDATION FOR DATING

Hi-Life Camp for high school youth group happened every summer. The theme of August 1985 was *Love, Sex and Dating*. I'll never forget it because I was so ready to get help in figuring this stuff out. Girls and guys separated for breakout sessions, and then came back together for co-ed sharing and discussion. Our leaders covered meaty topics from a Biblical foundation. They made it pertinent and fun for us passionate high schoolers. Some kids were already dating, and others were starting to pair up. The packed-out pages of journal notes I took are still valid today:

HI-LIFE CAMP
-Love, Sex + Dating-

"In order to have God's best in a dating relationship, we must first be the best that He wants us to be. The quality of a relationship is dependent upon the quality of the people involved. Here are seven qualities that you can seek to develop in your own life:

Commitment to Christ: The foundation of a relationship is spiritual. When one's life is committed to Christ, then can the whole relationship be committed to Him also (Romans 12:1-2). Christian relationships are different because they are based on the foundation of [a relationship with] Jesus Christ.

Acceptance of Self: There are some basic things that God has given to us that we do not have the power to change (Psalm 139:14-18). If we do not accept ourselves, we will have difficulty accepting others. When you can accept faults in yourself, then you can accept faults in others.

Harmony with Authority: Rebellion is a character trait that will manifest itself in a relationship. Learn to submit to authority now, and you will have less problems later (Romans 13:1-5). How I treat my dad is how I will treat my husband. I must learn to submit.

Clear Conscience – Freedom from guilt will allow for freedom of spirit and communication. You will feel free to respond to the needs of others (Acts 24:16). Guilt produces bitterness towards the other person. We must develop the ability to ask forgiveness and to forgive. We must have humility before God which will then transfer to our boyfriend/girlfriend/spouse.

Spirit of Forgiveness – There is always the need to ask forgiveness, but also the need to forgive. The ability to forgive will free one from bitterness (Ephesians 4:32). When you ask forgiveness, then you've already forgiven the other person in your heart. The ability to forgive and ask forgiveness shouldn't just start at marriage, but now in all your relationships. Habits are forming now that will <u>last</u>.

Moral Freedom – The battle for moral purity begins by taking control of the thought life (2 Corinthians 10:5). If the thoughts are pure, then so is the heart (Psalm 119:11). Habits developed now will continue into your marriage. G.I. – G.O. means "garbage in – garbage out." When we are tuned in to the Lord and walking with Him, filling our minds with things that would honor Him will cause us to endure under temptation. If we are practicing wrong things and filling our minds with sex and lust, we won't be able to resist temptation as well. Chances are, we will fail.

Purpose in Life – God saved us so that we may glorify Him (Ephesians 1:12). Our life goals as well as relationships should be governed by God's purpose for our lives. It's important to find someone with a purpose in life because he is going to be my spiritual leader. How can he lead if he has no purpose? How can I follow and trust myself to him if he has no idea what or where his life is going?

I must allow God to work in my life, realize my purpose, get my life right with the Lord and then the qualities I develop within myself will be what I look for in a date and these will set the foundation for a good marriage.

A RELATIONSHIP APPROVED UNTO GOD

In order to achieve God's best, a relationship must develop according to God's standards. Obeying God's order will result in a fulfilling marriage relationship, whereas a violation of God's order will lead to deeper problems and conflicts. The focus in a Christ-centered relationship is 'How can I help him in his Christian walk? How can I encourage, support, or help him to grow?' As a woman, my responsibility is to have purity and reflect purity. This is a spiritual challenge and encourages the guy to be a spiritual leader, which is his responsibility.

Dating is laying the groundwork for a marriage relationship. That means the spiritual emphasis should be the foundation, the whole focus, of a dating relationship."

God's Order   **Objectives to Achieve**

<u>SPIRIT</u>   COMING TOGETHER IN ONE SPIRIT:

Spiritual intimacy is achieved when two Christians can freely share their faith, devotional times, experiences, and prayers with one another. Genuine love is developed according to 1 Corinthians 13.

<u>SOUL</u>   MENTAL AND EMOTIONAL ONENESS:

At this level, likes and dislikes, strengths, and weaknesses volitional are learned. An understanding of habits and moods, etc. emotional is also developed. Acceptance of one another at this level is important. As the emotional bonds develop, temptation may become greater. That is why the need for spiritual intimacy comes first.

<u>BODY</u>   PHYSICAL UNION:

Physical intimacy is consummated in marriage. A fulfilling sex life is not limited to the physical but involves the total being – spirit, soul, + body. When physical involvement takes place before marriage, the spiritual intimacy is destroyed, and mental/emotional oneness is affected.

We went on during the next sessions to list *The Benefits and Dangers of Dating* and *What I Look for In the Opposite Sex*. Each gender came up with a list of almost twenty characteristics they were looking for in the other gender. That was eye opening for all of us! The leaders pointed out our need to focus on qualities we wanted in someone else, in ourselves first! Were we all those things we thought were so important?

THE JOY WEAVER - GRASSROOTS

The last two sessions of that glorious camp were *Ideas for Dates* and *Principles for Dating*. After brainstorming a list of eighty activities to do on a date, the list of *Principles for Dating* would have set anyone on a glowing pathway to success:

A) Establish a Friendship
B) Avoid Dating Unbelievers
C) Avoid Isolation
D) Plan Fun Dates
E) Dating is Preparation for Marriage
F) Avoid Getting Too Close Too Soon
G) Don't Stay Together Only For Security

All this teaching on *Love, Sex and Dating* sounded good and right and blessed. I grabbed up the part about working on myself to be a person worth dating. That seemed like a smart place to start. I earnestly intended to set my heart on Jesus more consistently. But imagining is not doing. My double-minded heart was still aching for validation in a dating partner. And before long, I would get my wish.

23 DOUBLE-MINDED

This balmy fall evening of junior year, inside and outside blended as breezes blew through sliders connecting the living room to backyard palms and starry night. A group of us from church and school were at our buddy's costumed birthday party enjoying munchies, laughter, games…and a dance. The boy in the white suit was wrapping gentle arms around me after an impatient friend had thrown us together. He was dressed as Don Johnson, the lead in Miami Vice. I had on pink dove shorts and a beach t-shirt after shedding my bag lady costume. I was in heaven, rocking back and forth to *Cherish the Love*, drawn up tighter to a boy than I'd ever been.

This mesmerizing moment had been meandering my way. Months ago, at a church family picnic, Brad had dunked me in the ocean before flirting with me in the waves and inviting me to play softball, which I did. As our group disbanded after an amiable afternoon, he had launched me disappointing news, "Bye! I'll be gone six weeks." Lamenting to my parents and John in the car piqued their interest! Brad's military family had been attending church, but our parents had not yet gotten acquainted.

By the time Hi-Life youth group convened for camp in August, Brad had returned as friendly as ever. I had tuned in to his answers during the coed discussions of love, sex, and dating. What was he looking for in a girl? What kind of dates did he think would be fun? Then I had ignored him for a few weeks because his hand had lingered on my leg after a scary scene at the movies with friends. I did not want to lead him on if I was not sure about him yet. Commitment was serious stuff! ...Here we were, now, reveling in this slow dance. Each stride was leading our hearts closer.

Following that event, Brad and I began talking on the phone, sitting together in church, and holding hands every chance we got. It became mostly obvious I was his girlfriend, and he was my boyfriend. I had to laugh when Mom asked in the car one day, "Are you guys chummy?" My brother had turned around in the front seat to grin at me. He knew what was up! "You could say that!" I answered brightly.

A couple of weeks after Brad and I had gotten together, I attended discipleship camp with the Servant Group of Hawaii Baptist Academy. We were about thirty Jesus-loving high schoolers wanting to make a difference with our faith. We spent time in worship, shared testimonies, traded encouragement notes and sat at a campfire talking, laughing, and building each other up. My camp-weekend roommate and I had prayed for God to use us for His glory – and both of us ended up listening, counseling, and praying with hurting classmates. We were so excited that we talked together in our room and praised the Lord, before crashing onto our pillows.

I was optimistic about managing life with a boyfriend while living hand in hand with Jesus. Thing is, I didn't know much about Brad's walk with Jesus. I prayed for the courage to bring it up. I guess the thrill of being liked had clouded my judgment.

Oct 1, 1985 I have a personal goal which fits in with my (new) relationship. I need to start having daily devotions and growing so that God can use me in greater ways. I believe that the ways He used me these past few days are showing me how much He can do with my life; so I need to prepare myself. I need to keep close to God so He can guide me and my boyfriend.

I've got to make sure this relationship never holds me back from growing closer to Jesus, from doing my best for God which means getting high grades in school, and I need to be positive in our relationship... I need to try and be serious with Brad and bring God into our relationship. Heavy stuff here, but crucial.

As near strangers – one fun kid drawn to another fun kid, our romance was mysterious in the beginning. Weeks turned into months, and we developed a very close friendship. Hundreds of face-to-face and phone conversations taught us a lot about each other. He was sporty and playful. But if he lost one of his football games, his silence suffocated me at times. Surrounded by cussing in his classes, he would let one loose now and then. "Don't talk like that," I would lecture, until I stopped acting like a mother. We exchanged funny stories about home life, such as his mom telling him I was too old for him (although she was nice to me). His parents expected him to conquer math challenges before he could get his driver's license, so I cheered him on. He didn't want to go on a single date unless he could drive us.

Other girlfriends had won his affections before me. He spoke of them frequently at first. It was unsettling, but I did want to know all about him. Our personalities were similar: gregarious, well-liked, and prone to being melancholy. We felt useful giving pep talks to our troubled friends, at church and each at school.

But rivalries were common in our youth group. I did not appreciate one girl who flirted with Brad right in front of me. She was standing beside him, "batting her eyelashes," when she wished out loud that she had a boyfriend just like him! Her actions made me miserable. Later, I would lecture myself, "Don't be jealous." But she seemed so out of line. How was I supposed to handle that? At least when girls invited him out, like to school dances, he refused them and said he had a girlfriend. Meanwhile, my journals describe my interactions with plenty of guy friends at school, too. We were both learning to be loyal.

Eventually our parents became friends. Brad and I usually sat with his family at church, unless one of us was late, and the pew was full. I was at his house often because his mom and dad hosted youth group events or stopovers on the way. His little brother would sit on my lap when I caught a ride with them (before the days of strict seatbelt laws). And my brother came on some of our outings, too. So Brad and I were growing together, and strong friendship was turning into real love.

My junior year was busy even outside of that relationship! Chatting and studying at church and school, working jobs at Burger King and babysitting, playing forward on the basketball team and treble clef in handbells. My parents grew weary of poking me, "Nancy, are you still tying up our only landline in the house? You are past your limit!" or "Are you still awake doing homework this late past midnight?"

I just had to journal before doing my homework most days. Amidst all the fun I had so much to process. I was worried, jealous, afraid of letting people down, venting, and asking questions, "Is he right for me?" I had many doubts and insecurities. Life was stressful. I was a yo-yo from happy to sad, fearful to courageous. I wrote to God about everything, but I did not know how to tune in and listen to His response. Or maybe I did not actually want to. God was like my old security blanket: cuddly, warm, and silent.

I had been given excellent teaching about developing a godly relationship. Yet thirteen months of dating without purposeful direction and accountability was turning into a murky mess of lukewarm love for God, disrespect toward parents, sloppy schoolwork, jealous friends, tarnished testimony and hands-on hypocrisy in cuddles and kisses. I desperately lacked self-discipline.

My will and emotions derailed me, as God's Spirit tugged me to get back on track. In the final weeks of our decaying relationship, I surrendered to the Lord. My boyfriend was one of my best friends! But our romance was rotten. It was finally clear to me we were never going to get better in it. Having begun on the wrong foot, without a firm foundation of commitment to Christ, we had crumbled. It was painful to break up. We both cried on the porch at church. And then I handed my whole heart back to God.

Galatians 5:16-17 *"But I say, walk by the Spirit and you will not carry out the desire of the flesh. For the flesh sets its desire against the Spirit, and the Spirit against the flesh; for these are in opposition to one another, so that you may not do the things that you please."*

1 Corinthians 6:18-20 *"Flee immorality. Every other sin that a man commits is outside the body, but the immoral man sins against his own body. Or do you not know that your body is a temple of the Holy Spirit who is in you, whom you have from God, and that you are not your own? For you have been bought with a price; therefore, glorify God in your body.*

24 HEARTACHE

(longing to be with the man God has for me)

This is a lonely moment
and I feel so lost inside.
I wish that I could cry a tear,
but it's just a waste of time.

'cause you're not here to hold me
or to tell me that you care.
And I don't even know you,
but you are around somewhere.

I pray for you at certain times,
though I cannot see your face.
And though our hearts are not yet one,
we both know God's hiding place.

And He will soothe my longing.
He will heal my saddened heart,
and draw me still yet closer
until of you I am a part.

So pray for me, as I for you,
then on that special day,
I'll know I'm yours and you are mine,
and that God has led the way.

Now I'm not so lonely.
My heart smiles deep inside,
because in His time we'll be together.
'Til then, in Him we will abide.

© February 16, 1987 Nancy

25 YOU COULDN'T PAY ME

College had seemed a long way off from the back seat of our car at the end of tenth grade. I was snug in my cozy family of four, barely halfway through high school. But I, as a visionary, with caring parents who readily dispensed wise counsel, had been discussing what I wanted to be when I grew up. I had declared my admiration for Dr. James Dobson and the heartfelt ministry of Focus on the Family. His testimony stated that God had asked him to relinquish his art career for a writing pen and degrees in psychology and counseling. He was already a PHD by the time I knew of him. We watched films of his in church like *Emotions: Can You Trust Them?* His books had helped me glean information I was too embarrassed to ask my parents about.

Sometimes, I imagined being the next-generation Dr. Dobson for struggling kids like me. It would be fulfilling to share God's love and Biblical wisdom with those suffering in sinful habits and trying to survive teen challenges. Dad told me no one gets a job as a counselor with only a four-year degree. I would have to start with a practical money-maker, like teaching. I could achieve my goal in stages, meanwhile supporting myself from a classroom.

Fast forward to Wednesday June 25, 1986, when our family boarded American Airlines Flight 34 in Honolulu and settled into our seats for the five-hour flight across the Pacific Ocean to LAX.

THE JOY WEAVER - GRASSROOTS

We were heading out on yet another summer home assignment right after my junior year. My college pick was still undetermined. I hoped to attend a big, quality, popular Christian college like Messiah in Pennsylvania, or Westmont College and Biola University in California.

Our annual Conservative Baptist National Conference was in July that year, at Colorado State University in Fort Collins. The adults attended one track of meetings, while teens attended their own gatherings. Bob, Marla, and I met and clicked quickly. We hardly stopped laughing the whole week. We sailed down giant slippery slides, climbed Rocky Mountains, and clicked our heels in the air swinging around a lamp post. Our silliest antic was laughing loudly at a droll part of a conversation, and then silencing abruptly with a frown that meant, "That was not funny!"

Late one night, after the speaker went to sleep in his dorm room, the three of us set to work on a practical joke. We filled dozens of Dixie cups with water from the drinking fountain and spread them out all over the hallway in front of his door. We were giggling and laughing, predicting how he might maneuver his exit the next morning. (He told us later that he had jumped.)

One of our meetings featured a concert presented by an ensemble from Southwestern Conservative Baptist Bible College in Phoenix, Arizona. The Chenaniah Singers traveled all summer, performing and recruiting applicants for the school. During intermission, they told us about Southwestern. Slides portrayed a lively campus of kids gathering in classrooms or hanging around outdoors. Academic degrees to choose from included teaching, missions, pastoring, and a couple others. College housing included one dorm and sixteen apartments. The student to teacher ratio was low. Wait…what did they say? Were there only 160+/- students enrolled in the whole school?

I was laughing again, in a mocking whisper this time. I leaned toward Marla's ear with a hand cupped over my mouth, "You couldn't pay me to go to a school that small!" The concert ended. The week ended. Bob, Marla, and I said our good-byes wistfully as we went our separate ways to rejoin our parents. TCK's are used to bonding and separating quickly.

Our family had a few weeks of road travel left together. My dad's parents had completed a pastorate in Chicago, Illinois and moved into a mobile home park in Ocala, Florida. We would spend a day or two nestled in their crowded home with the last of their earthly possessions tucked into corners and cupboards for retirement. MomMom played the organ for us and set my heart to reminiscing old hymns. I stood by their buffet cabinet and gazed at my favorite framed picture of them. It was 3-D, made with layers of cutout photos, stacked on glue dots.

When the sun peeked through the blinds of my guest room the next morning, I looked over the top of my bedsheets, marveling in a mysterious musical atmosphere. My ears heard nothing. My heart was full of wonder, joy, and peace. Was I soaking in angelic presence?

Later, as I stood at the trunk of our car, luggage loaded for departure, Grandpa Joe ventured a word with me. Southwestern College might be a good option worth praying about. He may have spoken of its affiliation with our Conservative Baptist Association, or the excellent price compared to bigger schools, or advice about listening to my parents. I was not thrilled with his ideas, but the warm wisdom of his deep voice sank into me like the butter on our breakfast toast. I might have to ponder it.

THE JOY WEAVER - GRASSROOTS

Back in Hawaii, the months were moving along. I needed to focus on real options. The mere cost of application fees would limit my number of attempts; but my pie-in-the-sky personality was still beaming big dreams. Mom and Dad suggested I talk with Mrs. Hirai, our guidance counselor at HBA. I had partnered with her on a work scholarship for several years. She was sweet as sugar and molasses. "Money matters," she sounded like Mom. "You cannot attend a school you cannot afford."

I applied to Southwestern and was awarded a four-year full-ride scholarship. I guess they would be paying me after all! I was grumpy about it at first. Why would an MK growing up in luscious Hawaii want to be dumped in the dry desert of Arizona with less kids than she was currently going to high school with? Still, I surrendered to the "blank check" deal from ninth grade. "If you want me to go to Southwestern, Lord, then help me to change my attitude." And slowly, but surely, He would.

Proverbs 16:3 *"Commit your works to the Lord, And your plans will be established."*

26 MY EARNEST PLEA

    Guy friends at school had all types of hair: straight black, wiry brown, wavy bleach blond, and dark whiskers. Taller or shorter, with various-sized muscles, glasses or braces, and straight or goofy grins. They could surf, sing, pray, write poetry, and preach. They dribbled down the court, lifted weights, played cards, mastered piano, learned to drive, and rubbed shoulders with brotherly love. What great men! Eligible bachelors spun my head and filled my heart with daydreams. Having torn away from my first love, I had escaped the probability of performing, but not the melodrama of male mania.

    Criss-crossed numbers on the calendar slowly shoved the rewinds of my painful breakup into the past. Now single, I was sleuthing the solution to my greatest unsolved mystery. Who would be my forever man? Where would I find him? Or would he find me? How would I know he was the one?

    For most of senior year I drew strength from and fostered fun with maturing groups of guys and girls at school and church. I had more time to spend with God, and more time for personal growth. My family liked me better, and I was better to them. Journal entries spoke in happier healthier tones.

<u>**Mar 2, 1987**</u> Things are going pretty awesome. I've probably had two bad days since I last wrote and both of them turned out good in the end...I've been doing so well since I've been single...I had a

wonderful week. Amy and I had devotions together and God answered many prayers.

I've had neat chances to witness at work, chances to share about mine or encourage others' Christian walks – with Amy, John my brother, my parents, guys at school. It's so neat! The more you put your faith in God and watch Him work in your life and then share that with others, the stronger you grow. John taught Sunday school this past week...shared from the heart. I'm so proud of my brother.

Then, after journaling about several friendly and entertaining interactions with guys, having been encouraged by each of them, I wrote:

You can see that by no means am I a lonely old maid. I'm not running around flirting either – I've just met some very nice guys who I'm getting to know and renewed some old friendships. I thank the Lord!

One of the new guys I was getting to know was stationed in Hawaii on military assignment and had started attending our church. Again? He wasn't the son of a military man; he was the military man. I was appreciating long-term friendships with a lot of guys at school and would be attending the Jr./Sr. Banquet with my heartthrob of sophomore year – still a dear friend. Meanwhile, the new guy had taken an interest.

Apr 16, 1987 He went to Korea and wrote me 4 letters while he was gone. I wrote to him too and we got quite a good little thing going. It gives me butterflies to think about it. He came back Apr. 14 (10 days early) and called me that night. It was so fun talking to him although I sounded terrible – I've been sick ever since I came back from my Senior Trip on Monday. He knew about my upcoming Jr./Sr. Banquet and told me he wanted a picture. "I'd love to see you all dressed up. I'm sure you'll be beautiful."

As we grew acquainted, and he proved sincere, I found myself very interested too!

Apr 20, 1987 I know I should be working on my paper, but I think another big part of my life has come along and I've got to get out my feelings on paper. I'm so excited I'm almost sick. He is all I can think about. He saw me yesterday at church and said I looked very pretty. We had so much fun talking. I sat by him morning and night and talked to him after church until leaving time both times. He gave me his jacket on the bench when it was raining, said he wants to come see our new house, is postponing his leave just so he can come to my graduation, offered me his shoulder when my neck got sore, asked for my new phone number and called me tonight. He's a Christian and we pray for each other and he's such a blast to talk to…He's got a really good heart, full of caring and concern and sincerity…I love him as a person. He's really neat! I'm just going to keep praying about the whole thing.

Outings and niceties increased. He would accompany us home, help on my school projects, dine with us, pay for my meals if we ate out, sit with me in church and phone me a few times weekly. He joined our youth group video scavenger hunt. He, my brother, my best friend, and I hiked Diamond Head and went shopping at the Ala Moana Shopping Center. He would hold on to hugs or my hand or smooch me on the cheek now and then. We were savoring a soft start in simple sentiments.

Yet everything and everyone I wholly cherished on my island home would soon diminish in the distance while I forged a future on the mainland. When I pondered missing meals and minutes with Mom, Dad and John, tears would trickle. My best friend at school, Amy, pulled off a surprise graduation party for me. The rowdy fun and loving laughter encouraged me and also intensified my sorrow as I saw faces of forever friends fading.

Therefore, when he gave me the valuable pearl mounted on a gold ring at the party, I took a step back and told him I could not commit long-term. He stayed near and dear anyway, right next to me at the church family picnic on the Fourth of July, watching fireworks fly over the ocean from seats on the sand. And on another day, I let him really kiss me.

Wait, what? Since our fondness for each other had not fizzled, we just kept hanging out. One afternoon, shortly before my scheduled departure to college, he had taken me on a lunch date. Dropping me off at my house, he was not in a hurry to say good-bye. As we stood in the kitchen, he leaned, I leaned, we leaned, comfortably connecting. But the worst thing happened! Sensing someone, I peeked over his shoulder and saw my brother shocked and embarrassed to have encountered us as he rounded the corner.

I jolted back and exclaimed John's name as he jetted from the scene. There was no magic left in that moment! It had been overwhelmed by awkward. After weirdly apologizing, I managed to say, "Thanks for taking me out," and saw him out the door. I knew in that moment that he wasn't the one, and "we" had hit a dead end. With a mere kiss?

Months of paper, pens, stamps, calls, conversations, church, family fun, gentle affection, dollars on dining, lively adventures, and dreamy drives had so suddenly reached "The End" - a perfectly good relationship? How did that make any sense? It had to be unfair to him. I had never meant to hurt him. I felt sick and sad. Now I was facing another hard conversation and another empty space in my heart. I went straight to my room, knelt by my bed, and poured out my fears and regret to the Lord.

My whole being was drowning in waves of repentance as I sensed a terror - that marrying the wrong guy was actually possible. One and done. One love for life. I could picture it - the complex permanence of "I do." "Till death do us part" could become scary and stuck if I wasn't positive God had written our names together in His plans. I began to plead, "Dear God, please don't ever let me marry the wrong man! And I don't want to "have to" kiss him first to find out I'm mistaken! And I pray You will let me be friends with the guy I'm going to marry for at least a year before I figure out that he's the one. In Jesus' Name, AMEN." I felt sick, but deeply relieved at the same time.

Slowly but surely, I was wising up about my absolute need to give God full control of my love life. I was tired of hurting people and tired of disappointing myself. I stood firmly on saving myself for marriage and staying married for life. Dating could wait!

2 Samuel 22:7 *"In my distress I called upon the Lord, Yes, I cried to my God; And from His temple He heard my voice, And my cry for help came into his ears*

27 BIG HOUSE - LOTS OF KIDS

My freshman through junior years of high school, Steve Murphy, or "Murph" as we liked to call him, was Christian Education Director at Hawaii Baptist Academy. He planned chapels, led a discipleship meeting once a week called Servant Group, hosted Servant Camp, and directed other spiritual-growth initiatives. His office was usually open for students to rest, eat, do homework, plan, pray, prank, or talk story. One day **I got a nuddy buddy and went to Murph's.** We harbored there on hundreds of occasions. If we needed one-on-one support, we received that as well.

As "Jesus in skin," he had helped me during two of my difficult moments. One day I was still tortured with tearfulness after weeping in the bathroom. Then, going to class, I kicked a cement post near the stairs and ripped a gaping hole in my nylons. The blood on my scraped shin matched my red high heels. I just could not get myself together. He could have looked the other way and passed by or cited me for being tardy. Instead, he came to me, asked what was wrong, listened and prayed.

The time I was tempted to drink until drunk with friends from church - one being my boyfriend, I ventured to ask Murph, "Why not?" If it was just one time in a safe place, without driving, "Would it be that bad?" No cut and dried clichés came from this wise counselor. With simple questions he led me to discover my own conclusion. Legally and morally, it was risky. My testimony would be tarnished. Parents would be angry. "But beyond that?" he nudged. Worse yet, I would sadden my Heavenly Father. My thoughts turned from law to love, and then my choice was clear.

There were other godly influencers at church. Our pastor's family took in a foster child named Mikey. Soon more families fostered kids, too. Some even adopted. Youth pastors and mentors were tireless in pursuit of growing us up to be solid Christians. They were perpetually present to preach, pray, and play. I grew in my walk with Jesus no matter what we were doing: sitting in the pew, singing in the choir, standing up in Bible Drills, holding babies in nursery, watching movies at home socials, eating at church picnics, or plugging my ears in a Stryper concert!

Russ and Ramona Simons came from the Philippines to give a presentation I would never forget. As dorm parents from Faith Academy, they explained what their job was like raising other peoples' kids during the school year. They made us role play various scenarios described on 3x5 cards passed out around the congregation. It sounded fascinating and fulfilling to me. Now Missionary Kid schools were on my radar as well. If I could not find a husband to dorm parent with, I could still teach!

The lives of all these people stood as beacons of potential career paths for me. I had been deeply impacted by these adults who loved kids, who knew how to have fun and still meet the demands of youth discipleship. And Dr. Dobson was continuing to speak to my questions and doubts, as he would for many years. Working with kids seemed to be a big part of my calling, and maybe missions would be too.

One day during senior year, I was chilling out in the Christian Education Director's office again. Mr. Murphy had been called to pastor a local church, so he was no longer there. The new guy was young, a single pastor from North Carolina. Ted Goslen would become one of my dearest friends for a while. He loved Jesus and he loved kids. He loved God's Word and he loved to have fun. His office was as full as ever; and he never seemed to mind the cacophony of rowdiness and wrestling.

But this day, still subject to emotional roller coasters, I had stooped to whining on the couch. I was bumming hard core because I could not figure out my future. Life after graduation was a mysterious mist. He asked, "Where do you want to be in 10 years?" I perked up. "All I know is that I want a big house with lots of kids!" That declaration stuck. He had helped me land on target at the heart of my dreams.

At my surprise graduation party, Mr. Goslen gave me a devotional with promises of God. In the cover he had written the reference **Proverbs 3:5-6.** *"Trust in the Lord with all your heart, And do not lean on your own understanding. In all your ways acknowledge Him, and He will make your paths straight."* Amy had put that passage on my graduation cake! I held these words in my heart as new life verses.

Day by day, as I acknowledged Him and trusted Him, the Lord would be faithful to lead me - to teaching, counseling, foster parenting, or dorm parenting – in a big house with lots of kids. And somewhere along the way, hopefully, to a husband!

28 TRANSITIONS

(reflecting as high school graduation approaches.)

It's a beautiful day in the neighborhood.
God made the world, and it is good -
from the children whose laughter is heard all around
to the beautiful nature that covers the ground.

I remember the swing set that my daddy made,
the homemade kitchen cabinet that on Christmas he gave -
the clothes and the dresses that my mommy sewed,
and the country Holly Hobbie that now is so old.

These thoughts aren't connected in any real way,
but they are the memories of long-ago days.
They make me thankful for my mom and dad.
Nowhere on earth could better parents be had.

And I think of my brother who's now a best friend.
I'd never have thought we'd get along in the end.
We used to bicker from morning 'til night.
Now there aren't many times we resort to a fight.

It's hard to believe that my childhood's at end,
and I'll never go through adolescence again.
I can no longer say, "When I grow up…."
'cause those days are here. Doesn't time ever stop?

THE JOY WEAVER - GRASSROOTS

I saw a commercial from American Airlines.
And it really hit me - it's just about time,
when I'll be the one leaving home on a plane,
heading toward college to fill up my brain.

© *April 10, 1987 Nancy*

29 THE NUT HOUSE

The handbook of Southwestern Conservative Baptist Bible College (SWC) read like a prison sentence as I was preparing to leave my happy home for a new life with strangers. Dress codes, curfews, co-ed restrictions in dorms, required chapel attendance and Christian service, and no public displays of affection (PDA) all sounded opposite of young adult fun and freedom. How was I going to enjoy my college experience in a place like that? I groaned and wept woefully on my bed.

The evening I landed in Arizona, I was picked up by one of the grown college kids my parents had befriended in Hawaii. "Peachy" was now pastoring a church. He drove me around "The Valley" telling stories throughout Scottsdale and Phoenix on our way to the school. We paused at a novel sub and slushie shop called *Eegies* to grab a bite to eat. I was welcome to attend his church, but I would not have my own car.

Less than a mile down Cactus Road, we had arrived. Taking a right turn, and then another, we proceeded around one quarter of the circle drive and parked in front of the only dorm - girls upstairs and guys downstairs. Having flown into the setting sun before landing, it was now dark in the desert. As if in a dry sauna, more than 100° swathed my skin. Besides a little traffic noise and crickets, campus was quiet.

Where was everyone? A car pulled up, and I was relieved to see signs of life. My roommate had come to greet me, hearing that the Hawaiian girl was showing up a couple days early. She was bummed to find I was not brown skinned with dark hair, like she had expected of a girl coming from the islands. I told how an Asian man on my flight had insisted I must be part Asian due to the almond shape of my brown eyes. There I was, not Asian, Hawaiian or even Hispanic; just 100% TCK.

Carolyn was delightful – an older student jumping in for a freshman year. She was bouncy and bright with a melodious chuckle that welcomed me in. Yet she only stayed for a moment. She had things to do and was not moving in until Sunday.

She and "Peachy" carried luggage upstairs and then departed. I was on my own! Seated on a bare bed I examined the simple surroundings – cement block walls, tile floors, popcorn ceiling…two beds, two closets, a long dresser/desk, and a sink. I blinked as the busyness of weeks was now in stark contrast to this silent solace. The blank canvas was soothing. All I had brought with me was bound in 10 square feet of space. I arranged it all in my new place until 3:45AM, near midnight in Hawaii.

At some point, I heard faint voices at the end of the hall. The Resident Assistant and her roommate were settled in, like they had been there all summer. Cindy toured me around the school – at least what there was of it. The administration building, with three classrooms and a library, sat like headquarters on the giant circular plot of grass in the middle of our property. South, across the circle drive at twelve o'clock, was a multi-purpose cafeteria where only M-F noon meals were available. We would fend for ourselves at other hungry times. A basketball court enclosed in tall chain-link fence was out behind the cafeteria. The portable east across the circle drive housed a science lab, restrooms, and music practice rooms.

Sixteen apartments, four per row, were lined up in stripes - with green yards, a tree or two and picnic tables in between. They sat on the southwest section. Three parking lots, two big fields, a baseball diamond, and a prayer chapel – that was it! Over the phone, recruiters had promised Mom the completion of a new facility with gym, chapel, classrooms, and a student center. I guess they had fudged their timeline since they had only graded the ground for it by the time I arrived.

Students trickled in Saturday and Sunday before orientation scooped us up to get acquainted. At the ice cream social, I was standing in a circle of new kids, all venturing to figure each other out. My eyebrows rose over a goofy grin after one girl spoke. "Wow! You're from Africa?!" I was verifying this amazing TCK discovery.

Looking stunned, Tonya replied, "No, Albuquerque." Argh; I had always struggled with my hearing after severe childhood ear infections. Eric, the pastor's kid from Washington, laughed loudly on the left. I felt dumb but did not let it lick my fun.

Monday night we were heading for western grub in the foothills. The girl from Albuquerque and I had worn pants! Having independently debated beforehand, since classes would require a dress or skirt, Tonya and I had each decided to take our chances for the social. When we saw each other on the dorm landing, we talked and laughed about it. Next moment, some guys pulled around in the circle below and said, "We have room for two!" Without thinking twice, we raised our hands and jumped at the opportunity, bounding unhindered down the stairs.

According to rumors, the cowboy restaurant would cut off and keep your tie if you wore one. Since our guys would be required to wear dress shirts and ties to class, they had donned dispensable ones from Good Will. We arrived at a gravel parking lot in the foothills of majestic purple mountains. Having chatted all throughout the car ride with our newfound friends, we ventured inside the rustic ranch building, walked across the hay-covered floor, and found seats together at a long wooden picnic table. While eating and enjoying our own vibrant banter, each fashion piece was scissored by rascally waiters and stapled in rows on the barn-like walls. Our laughter was not limited to the uproar of these shenanigans. We were pouring tea for each other, lifting pitchers as high in the air as possible, while filling our glasses to the brim. Tonya and I had chosen well – these would be friends for life.

That band of brothers became fondly known as "The Nut House." James, the Elder, was a senior music ministry major. James, the Younger, was a new believer freshman from Sierra Vista. Kevin was a pastoral major also from Sierra Vista, and Eric, the pastor's kid from Washington, was now interested in missions. Tonya and Sally, my neighbors in the dorm, rounded out the crew with me. Sally was an MK from Brazil who had grown up in boarding school. Tonya had been raised by devout parents with a Mennonite background. Our comradery in hundreds of campus life activities and adventures were lifegiving and inspired healthy maturation. We all loved the Lord and were preparing to serve Him. We were also young and silly.

By the sign that said, "Don't Feed the Ducks," we took photos of feathers hanging from our lips. Red Rover and human pyramids kept us entertained while we waited for friends to arrive at the airport. And we had to position a ladder at the second-story dorm window at 1AM because doors had been locked before we had returned from spring break. Seven of us would squish into a sedan to ride to church. Or we mangled melodies with *The Monster Mash* on cassette and flapped arms outside car windows like we could fly. Homemade pizza blessed our bellies after messing up the guys' apartment kitchen. And laughter over the movie

Princess Bride almost made us pee our pants! Waterskiing was wonderful and class pool parties cooled us off!

The Keirsey-Myers-Briggs inventory[13] helped us work well together. Volleyball and softball kept us running. I-10 and I-40 took us on the road for holiday visits or choir tours. We kept each other honest when writing papers and awake while we studied for tests. We became leaders in student government, on sports teams, and of music groups. We grappled with theology, evangelism, and missions. We experienced no shortage of prayerful encouragement and meaningful talks. Saying we had good clean fun would have been to say that the Salt River was just a bit wet!

But eventually, the whole group shifted. James the Elder graduated and married his fiancé from California. Eric and Sarah made a romantic deal for a foreseeable future. James, the Younger, and Tonya from Albuquerque started dating. My best bud from Sierra Vista welcomed his girlfriend to campus after she finished high school. Even my roommate, Carolyn, had started dating her future husband. All around me were pairs.

And I was still a single.

30 HIS HANDIWORK I SEE

Gems in the night sky caught my gander at a young age. "Look up," my dad would say, as early as the back yard in Tegucigalpa. Gazing into the blackness, alive with lights, I was especially keen on the radiant crisp white moon. Its curvature was easily visible around the edges, denoting a sphere. Way beyond Earth, yet near, it reflected sunlight from 93 million miles away. I marveled at the mysterious craters and varied colors evident on its landscape. We humans had recently set foot there!

God had made that moon! Though He Himself was imperceptible to my naked eye, I knew Him. He had forgiven me and saved me. I had been growing to know how much He loved me. His creation often wooed me. The stars were fascinating, forming pictures in the sky, or at least dot-to-dots of their "skeletons." I could see the North Star, the Big Dipper and the Little Dipper, and Orion. I especially loved Orion. His stark pattern was easy to pinpoint, and his stately form was not difficult to imagine. I loved admiring Creator God's canvas.

Some years later, on the island of Molokai, our family had accompanied my dad during the summer while he oversaw the construction of a radio tower. One night we were all standing out on a field, staring at the Milky Way. It was awe-inspiring to scan the massive cloudy white swath of myriads of millions of stars stretched across the sky like a heavenly highway. That is the first time I remember perceiving the full panorama.

A favorite hymn of mine at church, popular for singing around a campfire on retreats, was called *In the Stars His Handiwork I See*. The picturesque lyrics brought the bigness of a mighty God right into the warmth of intimate relationship with my feeble human heart. How could I so small unite with One so great?

During a tri-annual trip across the continental U.S., my family had stopped the car on a remote roadside well after sunset. I don't remember the reason, but what I do recall is seeing one of my first shooting stars. A small fiery ball blazed across the canopy of night before fizzling like the falling flash of a sparkler on the 4th of July.

A friend in high school youth group shared astronomical intelligence with those of us who appreciated being starstruck. He would lecture on the constellations located in the sky above Camp Timberline. Their names and meanings were beyond what I had heard about in childhood. I wondered how so many people could accept the preposterous lie that stars were steering them on and off course each day. I knew great balls of fire in perfect patterns were pretty, but not orchestrating life events!

The night before I left home for college, I stood on the driveway with my head tilted back. There was Orion. I admired him, standing peacefully firm in the face of all eternity. Knowing I would see this same constellation on the other side of the Pacific helped strengthen me for the long-distance leap to adulthood. Was I ready? The One who set those stars in place was accompanying me. I was going to be OK.

The first years of college, if I needed silence and solace at the day's end, I would saunter to the half-wall bordering our dorm parking lot. Nestled on a side street in a neighborhood, I felt perfectly safe. Lying on my back on the wall, with knees bent and arms folded around my ribcage, I was blanketed with any warmth leftover by the departed sun. From this darkness toward His light, my whispering worship wafted into His surpassing greatness in outer space. He was the One beyond everything. Simultaneously, I could be resting in His arms or leaning on his chest. If a shooting star flew by, I felt He was saying, "I see you. I love you. I'm here."

When Grandma Enid told me about the gospel being written in the stars, I was absolutely mind blown! I had shunned the teachings about the Zodiac as being tied to idolatry and fortune telling. The Sagittarius pillowcase my best friend embroidered for me in sixth grade had just "disappeared" not long after. I shuddered to think of resting my head on such a sinful subject. I avoided horoscope scrolls at the grocery store checkout lanes and was usually apprehensive about playful prods from fortune cookies. I saw all those things as Satan's trinkets, dragging the naive into a game that God did not want them to play – finding future, apart from Him.

Deuteronomy 4:19 *"And beware not to lift up your eyes to heaven and see the sun and the moon and the stars, all the host of heaven, and be drawn away and worship them and serve them, those which the Lord your God has allotted to all the peoples under the whole heaven."*

And that was just the thing, Grandma said. God had allotted the stars to all people under heaven, as a way of communicating with them from the very beginning. He, the First Born of all Creation, the Alpha and Omega, the Beginning and the End, had set His stars in the heavens as a sign. They were pointing the way to salvation, even before Eve's enemy, and ours, had slithered up to her seductively in Eden.

Grandma had discovered the ancient star chart swirling above our heads each night was depicting "twelve chapters in the heavenly story." Her information came from a new book called *The Real Meaning of the Zodiac* by Dr. James Kennedy (D. James Kennedy Ministries, © 1989). True revelation was readily evident if the star story commenced at the proper place. Before there was the book of Job, or the Torah written by Moses, there were prophecies, brilliantly portrayed on the portals of paradise, for all to see. Satan's servants had twisted the testimonies by torquing the treatment of the clue to "where it all began." In actuality by God's design, Virgo is the first! Leo is the last!

> Where do we begin to interpret this picture of the zodiac, since a circle has neither beginning nor ending? ...We may find the key to that riddle in the sphinx. I know it will surprise you, but the sphinx actually unlocks the mystery of the zodiac. It is fascinating to note that in the Temple of Esneh in Egypt, there is a great sky painting in the portico on the ceiling which shows the whole picture of the zodiac, with all of its constellations. Between the figures of Virgo, The Virgin, and Leo, The Lion, there is carved the figure of the sphinx with the head of a woman and the body of a lion. The word "Sphinx" means to "bind closely together." The Sphinx binds the two ends of the Zodiac together and shows where the great circle of the heavens begins and ends."[14]

Kennedy had demonstrated historically, archaeologically, anthropologically, astronomically, and Biblically that if the twelve signs are examined from beginning to end, they display the depths of God's plan with direct detail, to save His people from their sins and destroy Satan. *Ponder this! No other planet would perceive it the same way.*

Crazy curious about the specifics of this science brought back to light, I was handed the book to borrow for a few months. My faith had found another foothold. And I had adopted another method of testifying about the good news of Jesus Christ.

Genesis 1:16 *"God made the two great lights, the greater light to govern the day, and the lesser light to govern the night; He made the stars also."*

Genesis 15:5 *"And he* [the Lord] *took him* [Abraham] *outside and said, 'Now look toward the heavens, and count the stars, if you are able to count them.' And He said to him, 'So shall your descendants be.'"*

Romans 1:20 *"For since the creation of the world His invisible attributes, His eternal power and divine nature, have been clearly seen, being understood through what has been made, so that they are without excuse."*

31 THE LONELY YEAR

As all my friends paired off, I found myself alone in the dorm on Friday nights. Dating couples in duplicate or triplicate would picnic on the roof, find trendy spots in Scottsdale, or socialize late into the night. I still had friends who loved me. But a third, fifth or seventh wheel was lopsided. So I was the odd girl out on date night.

At times I would wonder if there were other people roaming campus looking for something to do. Excuses and extreme insecurity would drown out any thought of investigating. What if people rejected me? Would people think I was using them for the weekend while my "real friends" were busy? I preferred my best friends. If they were unavailable, it seemed easier, safer to stay in my dorm room alone.

My head would fill with depressing lies. Why could I not find a boyfriend? What was wrong with me? Was I boring, ugly, fat? These same questions had plagued me in high school whenever I found myself left out. Feeling sorry for myself was not helpful. The glum, energy-sucking, hopelessness weighed me down. I feared my despondent "blah" mood would slime someone. "Ew, it's no-fun Nancy!"

And then one night, lying listlessly on my bed, I heard Jesus, "You can date me!"

I was unimpressed by the suggestion, "'Cause that would be fun!"

He persisted, "I'm here for you. Spend time with Me! Read your Bible and pray."

I had been in church all my life, a Christian since I was six, and dedicated to God at fifteen. Yet the older I grew, the more uncomfortable I was becoming with His apparent game plan. How much was submission going to cost me? Why could all the others date a human honey while mine was hidden in The Rock? I wondered if He was expecting me to be forever single?! Sighing, I rolled over to grab my Bible.

Distractions made me a squirrely disciple, so time with Him was not a terrible idea. Admittedly, it was peaceful. Where would I start reading in my blue pocket Bible from Mom. Genesis? – I had been there many times. Philippians? - It was my old favorite. Proverbs? – Always practical. Psalms? I loved the Psalms.

David was a man of many mood swings so I could relate to him wholeheartedly! The ruggedly handsome shepherd and king refused to let struggles keep him down. It impressed me how he spoke so boldly and openly to God, His Father, with deep emotions, questions, and doubts. And then, after crying out about the hard stuff, David would sing a song of praise about the good stuff. David was an overcomer!

My own thoughts and feelings vacillated unpredictably, tethered to hormones, my circumstances, or both. A happy day could plumet to despair as fast as an amusement ride on the drop tower. An angry word could instantaneously burst from my lips like white puff from kernels in an air popper. Wistful daydreams rolled into lust if I was watching a romantic scene. Emotional zigzagging wearied me and my friends! As a verbal processor, I often brought them with me through tumultuous highs and lows.

Clearly, I needed help to stabilize my perspectives and interpretations.

Date nights with the Lord became valuable to me. I still relished big fun on campus or hoped for adventures with a future husband. But alone time with God was transforming my heart, mind, and soul to be secure in His love, and grounded in His truth. He helped me avoid sliding down slippery slopes of stinking thinking! And He helped me exercise more self-control in stressful situations no matter my mood.

Philippians 4:8 *"Finally, brethren, whatever is true, whatever is honorable, what-ever is right, whatever is pure, whatever is lovely, whatever is of good repute, if… any excellence…anything worthy of praise, let your mind dwell on these things."*

Romans 12:1-2 *"Therefore I urge you, brethren, by the mercies of God, to present your bodies a living and holy sacrifice, acceptable to God, which is your spiritual service of worship. And do not be conformed to this world, but be transformed by the renewing of your mind, so that you may prove what the will of God is, that which is good and acceptable and perfect."*

God was faithful to draw near to me as I drew near to Him. He was teaching me things I could not have learned if I had been swirling in satisfying social circles. He was moving in me to die to myself and be abundantly alive in Him - less old-man sin nature and more new-creation character in Christ. Above all, He was becoming my best friend for life. Lest it appear this was a smooth transition, bits and pieces of my journal portray the long road I walked over many months. I was often subject to great pain when I found myself alone…again, and again.

Apr 4, 1988 I was uneasy today because my friend told me that as she gets closer to her boyfriend, she wants him to be the one she tells everything to. I will still be her friend, but she wouldn't tell me all she does now. That's scary to me – it hurts.

    I do understand, but it leaves an ache in my heart and a knot in my throat. I just have to trust God to provide me with the friends I need. She's been so special its indescribable. When my best bud's girlfriend comes next year, I won't have my two closest confidants like I do now. I'm not complaining or being negative. I'm just expressing the hurt in my heart before my Abba Father. I've prayed before that God would do whatever it takes in my life to bring me completely into His will, even if it meant taking away my friends.

Sep 9, 1988 Help me experience victory in my Christian life and help me to learn to walk as an adult rather than stumbling about as a child.

Oct 8, 1988 Praise – I had a good Saturday night, though lonely

Oct 11, 1988 Life is truly awesome. I've kept reading in Genesis, and I've been developing an attitude of prayer. When I feel my mood drop, I'm reminded of my joy in the Lord and that contentment doesn't rest on circumstances. So I've been stable.

    Even though Saturday night I was left alone and was angry, the Lord listened to me cry in frustration, then pushed me to do something constructive. I sang and then walked around the circle listening to my Walkman. I almost walked myself to sleep. Anyway, the Lord is always with me, and I can feel Him working in my life again. I feel content and able to rejoice, ready for life, ALIVE!! Thank you, Lord Jesus, for being my father, for giving me life and freedom – wow – such a freedom. What made you give up so much for someone so little?

Oct 28, 1988 I'm feeling restless, maybe still lonely – but I'm not going to let it affect me. The Lord has much growing for me to do. I keep spending time in His Word and being joyful in my salvation, and all that God has provided for me.

It's hard – I'm not trying to cover up that fact. At times I feel incapacitated in my relationships with people, and there are still times I cry – But I know down deep in my heart that God is faithful. His love is unfailing. As long as I cling to Him, He will be sure to meet all my needs - YES, even mental and emotional.

I wonder how often Jesus felt all alone and saddened during his life on Earth. I'm sure it hurt Him too, to have His people turn away and not understand...

O God, please fill my loneliness. I cry out to you from a hurting heart that is unsoothed. Please help me to find my comfort in your love. Please help me to be pleasing to you even when I feel so all alone. Please help me not to blame anyone. Please help me to reflect your love and peace even in difficult times.

Personal Prayer List
-to be sensitive to hurting people - be willing to go out of my way to encourage
-consistency in prayer life and devotional walk
-allow the Holy Spirit to have full control

THE JOY WEAVER - GRASSROOTS

Nov 6, 1988 This morning I was thinking about all the time I spend in my room and that it was neat when a girl came by a few times a couple of weeks ago. I thought about how always being in my room could make me available to help people or be there for anyone who needs to talk or borrow something or get help with homework. So I prayed casually about it this morning. And tonight, another girl – who I almost never see or talk to, and who knows many others better than she knows me – called to ask for help on her homework. I thought that was a really neat answer to prayer.

Nov 14, 1988 Today's been kind of weird. I'm moody – don't know why. But classes are out and now I'm on the lawn about to do homework. I'm listening to my Walkman - PSALMS ALIVE. The air is cool, the grass is cool, and the sky is blue and it's a beautiful day. I belong to the Lord and He's still working on me. So even on the rough days I can smile and leave everything in His hands. Thanks for lifting me up, Lord. You are always a reason to rejoice, and you are always worthy to be praised!! ☺ ☺ ☺ ☺   I love you, Lord, because of who you are!!

    Psalms 5-14 I read to bring my spirit up. It's comforting and encouraging to see how David felt down at times, and yet He too drew near to the Lord and praised Him and always came to know that God would bring him through.

Nov 18, 1988 Went to Dorothy's for dinner at the retirement center behind Southwestern, and she showed me pictures and told me about her husband's death. She's lonely – I should go over there more often... Then I wanted to look at the stars, so I laid on a picnic table behind the cafeteria and prayed and prayed for sooo many people and situations and praised God. At 11:00 I was frozen stiff and went inside.

Nov 19, 1988 A group of dating pairs were playing Pictionary over in the cafeteria. Alone in the dorm, I cut pictures out of magazines, hung up new things on the wall, cleaned our room and did laundry. Meanwhile, the group had gone to someone's house to watch a movie. I cried. I don't like being left alone all the time on weekends; but I put on a Steve Green tape and prayed and soon felt better. I decided to call my brother.

The girls came home a little before midnight. They were in our dorm room talking, and I was in the hall on the payphone with John. When I came back to the room, two of them got up immediately and left. I felt so out of their group. I know I shouldn't. But 95% of the girls on our floor are going out with someone. I just don't feel like I fit in. I went to bed and cried myself to sleep, praying.

Dec 4, 1988 Lord, Monday I went literally crazy with frustration. You saw me. God, it scares me. Tonight, MaryLou told me about how her friend had just had a nervous breakdown. What scared me were the symptoms. They sounded like me. I don't mean to make a big deal except it really did scare me, Lord. Please hold on to me.

Help me to know you love me even when I lose control...I need to rid myself of unreasonable expectations and feeling guilty when I can't do it all – and you don't ask me to. Help me to know the things you want me to do – the things you consider important – and help me to say no to the rest without feeling bad about it.

THE JOY WEAVER - GRASSROOTS

I need to realize my limitations. I don't want to be overzealous and stress out so badly that I'm unstable and unusable. Thanks for my talk with MaryLou.

Jan 27, 1989 Found Paula looking distraught in the afternoon and ended up talking to her for an hour and a half. She was down because she felt so lonely. I marveled.

Her feelings mirrored my own from last semester. 2 Cor. 1:3-4 came to mind. God is amazing. Normally I have so many people to talk to and so much going on that I would not have empathized or taken the time to genuinely care.

2 Corinthians 1:3-4 *"Blessed be the God and Father of our Lord Jesus Christ, the Father of mercies and God of all comfort, who comforts us in all our affliction so that we will be able to comfort those who are in any affliction with the comfort with which we ourselves are comforted by God."*

Jan 30, 1989 LONELINESS. Last semester was tough, but I spent many hours in prayer and singing and being on my own. I was lonely through Wednesday. Thursday woke up feeling very oppressed. I began to pray, and the Lord lifted me up and made me feel glad again, determined to go through each day seeking His will.

As I isolated less, dates with God moved outside. Worshiping with my Walkman on the track or under the stars brought me into His presence. Favorite albums were Russ Taff *The Way Home*, Maranatha praise, Steve Green *Hide 'em in Your Heart*, and Keith Green *Volumes 1 & 2*. Exercise with God was an effective means of managing my stress. I'm sure He was smiling there on the b-ball court if I splashed three points or cheered if I swished for two. If I was overzealous or angry for some reason, I would run vigorous layups, or jump up to kick the chain link fence with my feet. Yet I would never feel alone again out there *with God as my best friend!*

The following semester was so much more enjoyable! God had drawn me to Himself. As my best friend for life, Jesus had given me new friends in addition to first friends. MaryLou, Paula and I were always busy with something!

We talked, shopped, cooked, walked, and worshiped. We built a Taj Mahal for the mission conference and planned the Fall Festival. We had fun with guys, shared a ton of homemade cookies, and most importantly, we prayed! Tonya, Sally, and I had been huddling up for prayer since the year before using 3 x 5 cards which listed requests and answers to prayer. The results had been encouraging, so we kept right on meeting! MaryLou and I would stop what we were doing and pray, in and around daily life, as needed. And Paula and I scheduled to meet and pray weekly.

Slowly but surely, I gained victory in emotionally unstable scenarios that formerly would have sent me spiraling into miserable frustration. One morning, walking on the path from our dorm toward the classrooms, I felt rotten. Like a bucking bronco, my thoughts and emotions were tossing me all over the place.

James 4:7-8 says, *"Submit therefore to God. Resist the devil and he will flee from you. Draw near to God and He will draw near to you..."* Taking up the reigns of my authority in Christ, I covered my mouth and spoke a rebuke against the one who comes to steal, kill, and destroy our peace of mind and productivity. In a Spirit-led challenge, I removed that burr from my saddle and remained confidently seated with Christ.

Another day during a biology lab, I panicked over pigs! We were dissecting brain and intestines of a fetal pig. Usually not squeamish, I don't know what set me off. As my partner and I cut back the scalp, opened the skull and poked near the brain, I lost it. I went to the bathroom where I was hyperventilating. Up to that point, I had never suffered a panic attack. The Holy Spirit directed me to recite all the Bible verses I knew. He used God's Word to bring my heart, soul, mind, and body into perfect peace on solid ground. I regained composure and laughed about it later!

Psalm 61:1-4 *"Hear my cry, O God; Give heed to my prayer. From the end of the earth I call to You when my heart is faint; Lead me to the rock that is higher than I. For you have been a refuge for me, a tower of strength against the enemy. Let me dwell in your tent forever. Let me take refuge in the shelter of Your wings."*

Thanks to God, He led me through "the lonely year" in the way I needed to grow – abiding in Him! He had been using the time to develop my character and anchor my identity in His love. I came to know I was never alone! I could always have a date! I did still wonder if His plans included allowing me to get married!

32 NEW SONG

When your spirit's overflowing
with honor and with praise,
do not quench its yearning –
let heart and voice be raised.

Father God, Almighty,
you are the only one
worthy of our praises
and honor to the Son.

My mind just cannot fathom,
my spirit can't endure
the awesomeness of your love,
your forgiveness always sure.

How can I be so ungrateful?
How can I refuse your will?
How can I pass a single day
without making time to be still?

Father, purify this heart of mine –
rip out those parts unclean.
Renovate my selfish life -
of other's needs make me keen.

I cannot stand to think, Dear God,
that the days go by a waste.
Father, bring your cleansing love –
mold me, make me chaste.

THE JOY WEAVER - GRASSROOTS

Aware of only needy,
compassionate toward the lost,
willing to lay down my life
obedient, regardless of the cost.

O Father God, I love you!
But my spirit wars the flesh.
Create in me a clean heart.
Make my commitment fresh.

O Father God, I love you!
Enslave me to your cause.
Teach me to surrender
until you are Lord of all.

© May 25, 1989 Nancy

33 BIG BEAR BURDEN

Pine Summit Christian Camp in Big Bear, CA had hired me to be an elementary camp counselor. There would be no time to return to Hawaii that summer. When the last sun set on my sophomore year of college classes, I flew from Phoenix, AZ to Ontario, CA. As I walked off the plane into a new-to-me airport, I began to look for other staff members who were also just arriving. Searching for strangers in an unfamiliar terminal was confusing but amusing! We didn't have smart phones in those days. When we had located each other, we piled into a car. An eighty-minute drive, climbing six thousand feet on a mountainous serpentine highway facilitated our friendships. Eventually, we rolled into a small town, nestled in the thick woods of San Bernadino National Forest, near the southeast end of Big Bear Lake.

The town of Big Bear and Pine Summit Camp were a camper's wonderland! The vast array of outdoor activities would be as fun to learn as they would be to teach the kids! Big Bear boasted canoeing, catamarans, horseback riding, alpine slides, hiking, and biking. The hilly campgrounds were shaded by Manzanitas and Jeffrey Pines. They hosted orienteering, air rifles, wrist rockets, archery, arts and crafts, swimming, and campouts under the stars with hobo dinners roasted on campfires.

Rhonda was my staff roommate and became my closest friend. We burped aloud, played practical jokes, shared boy stories, and continually cracked ourselves up. We also enjoyed discussing the Bible and sharing prayer requests. I was amazed at how many girls prayed to receive Christ as Savior during her cabin devotion times! If one of us was sick, the other would help cover responsibilities. We were a team!

Frontier Junction was for elementary kids. My first campers that summer were Kendra, Erin, and Lisa. After being introduced and chatting a bit, we marched up the hill to our cabin in the woods without plumbing or heat. We settled in and then returned to join everyone for the opening ceremony. So much joking and jostling!

Each morning, I woke before the girls to make a shower trek and have quiet time with the Lord. Breakfast before chapel gave us stamina to last through rotations of activities. After lunch we played big group Shenanigans: Octopus and Kick the Can on the field, or Paul Revere, Gold Rush, and Pony Express in the hilly forest. Days wound down at the Hickory Fire Pit with skits, *Boom Chick-a Boom* or *Bear Hunt,* and campfire songs. Back at the cabin and ready for bed, we would reflect, share, and pray together. Ministering to these growing girls was fulfilling!

On days off we joined other staff buddies to go hiking, sailing, or waterskiing. Rhonda's old beat-up white car would puff clouds of diesel exhaust as we drove around the lake through town. After campers left on Saturdays, we'd wash clothes at the laundromat, and then head to Thrifty's to buy snacks, supplies and ice cream. On Sunday mornings we would attend one of the local churches, trying out a few different ones that summer. Following 24 weekend-hours off, staff would meet in Town Hall for praise and prayer and to prepare for the next wave of kids.

Every few weeks, camp counselors became support staff for a restful change of pace. On Munchkin Patrol, we searched for lost or straggling kids. On dining hall duty, we might serve scrambled eggs, cinnamon rolls, or oatmeal. Then we'd lead activities like crafts, archery, or air rifles. After lunch, we ran errands in town or performed random jobs like cleaning and packing for Director Cheri, who needed to move. At night we'd hike near the cabins ensuring that campers had gone to bed. On-duty counselors might roll their eyes at us, envious of our freedom! When tasks were over, we'd hang out a while in Tamarack Lodge for co-ed goof off fun. Then we'd bid goodnight and cozy up in our own warm rooms with indoor plumbing.

In mid-summer, Pine Summit Camp had prepared to host high school kids for a week. They were coming from many different churches with their own counselors. Rick and Mick had been invited as special guest speakers for chapel. The activity stations and Shenanigans had been adjusted to suit older kids. Rhonda and I, as support staff, were at the registration tables helping the new arrivals to check in.

Next thing I knew, Director Cheri had come to me, "Nancy, a group of girls is here without a counselor. At age 20, you are the oldest available staff member. I need you to fill in." Suddenly, my "free" week had been traded for full-time duties with kids not much younger than me. I was annoyed; but worse, I was terrified! I struggled incessantly with insecurity and often felt like a nerd. How was I going to lead a group of girls who might not like me? Was there any way I could get out of this?

After our first assembly meeting, having made no real connection with the girls yet, I did the only reasonable thing I knew to do – run for the bathroom! I sat in the corner and cried and prayed. Eventually, Cheri and Rhonda found me there in the handicap stall and sat on the floor to comfort me and cheer me on. "You can do this!" Rhonda said. "God has a plan for you!" Cheri said. I begged to get out of it, but resistance was futile. God had called my number and these godly women were not going to let me miss an opportunity to stretch beyond my fragile comfort zone.

Then instantly, our world went dark! Stan, the janitor, had turned out the lights, not realizing that people were still in the bathroom! The comic relief of our boisterous belly laughter gave me joyful courage I needed to face the daunting challenge.

Jul 9, 1989 Have to rely completely on God. I feel weak.

Jul 11, 1989 I have never had to pray with such complete helplessness, with such complete reliance upon God to work in lives, to give me courage to stand for Him and to love these girls, not seek their acceptance. 'For I am not ashamed of the gospel of Christ, for it is the power of God unto salvation.' (Romans 1:16) Vicki, the coun-selor of the other girls is a big support. We have talked and prayed and pleaded with the Holy Spirit to move in the lives of these girls. This is a tough week, but God is having His way in my life, and I'm excited for what He is teaching me.

July 14, 1989 This week has been a monumental lesson in my life. Sunday I was on support staff when three girls showed up without a counselor. I was asked to be their counselor. I was disappointed, scared, terrified, struggling. I asked the Lord for strength because I knew He had a purpose for putting me in this position. But I felt such feelings of inadequacy, me being 20 years to their 15, and not making an easy transition from "mom" at Frontier Junction to "friend" at the high school level...

My three girls are neat. I sat down with them Sunday night and told them I was a bit (ha!) nervous and that I wanted to have a good week and I wanted to be their friend. This has been the most spiritually exciting week. The Lord has drawn me so close and caused me to put my trust in Him every second. Being disciplinarian was hard, but I believe I gained their respect. I love each of them and they love me. They've grown this week, and I believe God has accomplished His will in their lives.

During my senior year of high school at HBA, I had verbalized my ten-year goal in answer to my Christian Education Director, Ted Goslen. I had imagined myself as a dorm mom or foster mom in "a big house with lots of kids." Somehow, I had not pondered the process of growth and development necessary to prepare me for that God-given dream. This week with high school girls became one deposit toward the cost of "full surrender" which I had agreed to on that ninth-grade blank check.

34 THE POWER OF PRAYER AND PRAISE

> My Jesus!
> You are Sovereign.
> You have heard each prayer.
> And I've been astounded
> by the lessons you have shared
> with a girl who so often
> forgets you are Lord.
> Yet you bless me with answers
> of your own accord.
> Jesus, I bless You!
> Your Name is so sweet.
> Without you within me
> I'd be incomplete!
>
> © *January 29, 1990 Nancy*

In the fall of 1989, a dream and discussion from spring semester was becoming a reality. It was the birth of a student-led praise band created to volunteer in churches who did not have their own worship teams. Jared, the lead organizer, had several goals for the group: Part of our purpose through the band ministry is to have an expectant attitude and be contagious at school (SWC). We also envisioned exposing traditional churches to modern worship, inspiring them to start their own groups. He and I had been casually singing and praying together since last semester and looked forward to strengthening others with the joy we were finding in the nearness of God. Four to five of us began practicing each week and prayed Jesus would lead us to connections and open doors to minister. And God began to move!

Needs came up slowly at first: a Sunday in a Lutheran church, a Wednesday evening at the Phoenix Rescue Mission, a Saturday night at First Christian Church's youth event, and a weekend youth rally in Globe, led by good friends, Nathan and his fiancé, Trudy. The head pastor there had discussed with us the viability of various instruments for worship. (Many traditional churches at that time were opposed to electric guitars and drums.) Our hope of being used as a catalyst was being met.

By spring of 1990, the praise band was busier than ever. Many Sundays we helped Pastor Glenn at his growing church in Mesa. Sometimes we were asked to play for SWC chapel. We had been recruited to serve Wednesday nights at the college Bible study of Scottsdale Baptist Church. Donations for band and sound equipment had even been given to our team leader. And our band was growing! At first it was Jared with his guitar, our drummer Andy, and Kyle playing electric guitar. Andy's sister, Randi, and I were vocalists. A few more members would be joining us soon!

Meanwhile, student life was rolling along like a mini revival. Andy was mentoring freshman guys. I was encouraging newcomer Kelsey like a brother, cheering him on in his commitment to memorize Scripture and not to date. Paula, Randi, and I were praying together, as were Sally, Tonya, and I, and MaryLou, too. Quiet time was now part of my more disciplined routine. I looked forward to it!

My journal pages were flooding with answers to prayer and stories of God's work in many of our lives, including my family. John was a sophomore at the United States Air Force Academy

(USAFA). God was strengthening his faith through trials and temptations. My parents would soon return to Hawaii, having been on the mainland for home assignment, seeking renewed provisions of finances and prayer. They had managed their travels in a troubled borrowed car! And then finally…

Jan 5, 1990 I have a car! After a whole year of catching rides, using my bike, and sticking to jobs and ministries on campus, riding buses to places, and trying to be patient when Dad said wait, You, God, provided us with a perfect deal!

Jan 9, 1990 Your Spirit told me my grumpy friend was under stress, that she needed love and concern. When I talked to her, sure enough; she was stressed about a job and finances. I'm grateful, Lord, you helped me be a friend instead of judging her.

Jan 10, 1990 Mom and Dad were very late meeting me, and I was starting to get upset. But suddenly You told me You wanted me to be patient and not to be bothered by little things. I prayed for help to be patient and to not make cutting remarks. Then I sensed they were coming and looked up to see them on their way down the street. And the moment I saw them, I completely forgot about asking why they were late!

Jan 11, 1990 I was praying in the chapel and the Holy Spirit just prayed through me. I felt convicted to pray specifically for a job with kids and that I would get one soon. The next morning God sent a friend to tell me about P.A.L.S. (an after-school care program for elementary kids) and that day God just landed me the job!

Jan 14, 1990 I prayed this morning that God would teach me in church and "boy!" did He ever. I eat up the sermons. And I met more new college people today.

God has also answered my prayer for more female fellowship, and I am grateful. I've been less concerned with guys. (I had very strong feelings for the band leader.)

Paula, Randi, and I turned down "free" desert at Denny's from a waiter, in standing for our Christian faith, because it would have been dishonest. We were trying to be nice and are praying for his salvation. Thanks Lord, for helping us to take a stand. Please bring him into your family and allow him to feel your love and grace!

Jan 15, 1990 Paula, Randi and I met to pray for our first time. We're excited about what God is going to do this semester. Again, I praise God for good girlfriends and help with getting guys out of my mind.

John called and God is teaching him to pray for others when he is tempted. What a great counterattack! (...when the enemy comes expecting him to fail).

Jan 17, 1990 Bible study at Scottsdale Baptist was neat. I had prayed that God would be glorified and that He would help me reach out to people. It was a neat evening. I was not self-conscious and reached out to people even if they did not come to me.

One college guy shared how awesome it was having a praise band and how they had prayed for one. So I was excited that God is using us to answer that prayer.

Jan 18, 1990 The Lord helped me to buckle down at work because these kids need discipline! Even with all the hassles, the Lord helped me, and I am still loving the job.

THE JOY WEAVER - GRASSROOTS

Jan 19, 1990 The Lord helped everything to go quickly and smoothly so I was able to take care of fingerprinting at the police department and notarization at the bank for my Day Care Worker registration.

Our church college group went on Operation Love. There were more people than I expected. This was an answer to prayer, after only five of us went last November to The Ronald McDonald House. The leader came up and encouraged me when I was feeling out of place. Even though I'm really busy this year, I can do my small part.

Jan 20-21, 1990 the Praise Band had an awesome time at the youth rally in Globe. God was glorified and we had a fun time worshiping together. One of the needy kids won the Bible drawing. And Jared had prayed that God would make that happen for him.

Then came the start day of the most monumental answer to my prayers in years, though I had no way of knowing it yet! On this day, of this journal entry, it was as if Jesus set a timer for an official countdown in heaven. 52 weeks... 1 year...

Jan 22, 1990 I was thinking **Monday** or so about how I prayed so long for a job and a car and always had these aesthetic impressions of what I needed/wanted, and God answered my prayers in full. Not that my car is perfect because it had the smoky smell and a few squeaks, not the job either because the kids are out of control. But I love both and they fit the aesthetic sense I had of them.

I believe it will be the same with my husband because I have the same type of aesthetic sense. And I realize he won't be perfect, but he will be perfect for me – God's answer to my prayers for a loving, godly man in full.

Not knowing anything unique was afoot, I blew right on by, marveling at all of God's answers to prayer month after month.

There were opportunities to witness in restaurants and at work. There was the night Paula and I had both felt compelled to pray for my brother. Turns out that a classmate at USAFA had talked with him about the Lord for 2 ½ hours that very evening!

The praise band received additional donations, and more open doors to lead worship. My buddy Tonya was waking up already in prayer each morning. She was reading her Bible for hours at a time and memorizing huge sections. God was on the move, and we loved Him!

35 A BOY NAMED BILL MCCOMB

On February 1, 1990, Sally told me about a conversation with Eric earlier that evening, "Eric told me that he and Bill McComb had a chance to talk tonight about missions, and how God can use people. He said the guys are meeting in the dorm spontaneously for prayer. It just seems God is working." I responded, "I'll say!"

I didn't know Bill McComb hardly at all, but I knew he had started school with us in the fall as a freshman with Kelsey, Larry, Phil, and others. He had lived at home and drove a white Datsun truck. When it broke down irreparably, he traded a gas pedal for bike pedals to cover the eight miles from his house! He finally figured out a way to live on campus and moved into the dorm as another Bill's roommate. I knew he was downstairs; I just hadn't had occasion to talk with him much.

Two days later, Bill McComb approached me about the praise band. He attended the college group Bible study where we played on Wednesday nights. Bill said the leaders at Scottsdale Baptist wanted us to add male vocals and a keyboard. He suggested we talk to Phil. Since Jared had talked to Phil that very day, we were all set!

By mid-February, Bill McComb was mingling in the same group I was. I put him on my prayer list with the freshman guys downstairs, and often wrote his full name so as not to mix him up with his roommate. Even Bill McComb's parents were on my prayer list in mid-March. I was joining him in asking God for their salvation.

Mar 4, 1990 Bill asked me to go to church with him. I was in a dilemma – the band leader and his friends were coming by... I had wanted to bake cookies for them. But I did not feel like hanging on to notions of him. I wanted to go to church. The Lord told me to go to church, so I left Jared a note and got ready. Church was good. Heritage Singers came, and it was worshipful. Bill and I sang along with Keith Green in the car and talked in between. I wasn't nervous at all - I think we'll have a neat friendship.

Mar 5, 1990 Bill and Kelsey were my alarm this morning throwing rocks at my window. I got up and went to the window – definitely nothing like Rapunzel – I had just woken up ☺. But I sat on my desk talking to them for quite a while and then came in and got dressed for the day. I took them down some cookies I baked last night. Having open dorms is fun. I talked to them for ½ hour and then came back upstairs.

Mar 7, 1990 I climbed Camelback this morning with Bill McComb. Great exercise – left me a bit shaky. He's a nice guy but we never have much to talk about – made me miss the gang. (Normally a big group of us went. The guys usually ran!)

Abruptly, he dropped off the tip of my pen and ink radar for two months. Maybe he had noted I was still tangled up in a barren relationship, going nowhere. I was surrendered in the madness, praying about it often, wondering what to do. It was a hard place to escape from because the leader of the band and I had been friends a long time now. At the beginning of May, Bill surfaced again in a brand-new spot.

May 2, 1990 Bill, Deb, Karen, Jared, and I prayed again at Jared's house. It was great getting together and being in the Lord's presence.

Herein lies the evidence of something I never wrote down. Somewhere along the way, in the middle of spring, Bill had talked to me at the back door of the downstairs dorm one afternoon. "I'd like to join the praise band," he said. "I sing bass." Still stuck in my bedraggled infatuation with the band leader, I had answered coolly, "I'll have to talk to Jared." I did ask him, and he agreed to have Bill join us.

And since Bill attended Scottsdale Baptist Church where the praise band had been serving on Wednesday nights, and since he did not have a car, he often asked me if we could drive together. He was a neat guy with a new strong love for Christ. And he was chill – happy to be himself. He never seemed worried or embarrassed. He was funny! And sometimes he was just as happy to hang out with nothing to say.

My memories of those car rides are of us singing together, and sometimes talking. He had listened to heavy metal as a non-Christian. Yet now he enjoyed softer, worshipful melodies and heartfelt praise. *One God* was a favorite we harmonized with.

Hear O Israel, the Lord our God is One God. Hallelujah! Ha-lle-lu-jah!
Hear O Israel, the Lord our God is One God, Hallelujah!
And thou shalt love the Lord thy God with all thy heart
and all thy might,

Nancy McComb

Give Him glory, King of glory, In His ways delight.
There is no other Savior, no other life Redeemer.
We give our all to praise You and lift our voice in declaration.
Hear O Israel, the Lord our God is One God. Hallelujah![15]

One evening, we were driving along, talking about devotions. I don't know anything else specific about the conversation. What I remember is a faint fleeting thought as we crossed over a speed bump, "I wonder if I'll marry him someday." It was so subtle that I'm not even sure what the exact words were. All I know is that the moment whispered by, and we kept riding along as if I hadn't thought a thing.

36 BEST FRIEND TO THE RESCUE

I was going where no me had ever gone before. And it felt super. Last summer I had worked at Pine Summit Christian Camp in California. This summer I would be working at Camp Algonquin in northern Wisconsin. Last summer I had served in a familiar setting. This summer I was looking forward to a new challenge. Last summer I had been hired to tell kids about Jesus. This summer I might be the only one knowing Him. Last summer I had been "just across" the Pacific Ocean from home in Hawaii. This summer I would be 4,156 miles from Oahu by plane ride, bus ride, car ride and on foot into the woods surrounding Rhinelander - as a total stranger.

Mom and Dad were not thrilled. It was nowhere and with no one they knew. There was no connection to family, friends, or churches; they were hesitant! My friend Jared at Southwestern, the praise band leader, hailed from Wisconsin. He had suggested it. He had worked there in the past and felt I would enjoy the opportunity to witness for Christ. Yet without a support network, I would be taking a huge risk. Was my faith strong enough to endure the secular heat of summer? Would I make wise choices and lead people to Jesus? I sure wanted to try. Being a junior in college, Mom and Dad offered input while giving me freedom to formulate a decision. I talked to God about my choice at great length. I wanted to know what He wanted.

Feb 20, 1990 *God, I wish you could just tell me! I can't make decisions based on feelings! How can you let me wonder so unknowingly - can't you tell me something?*

This morning I read <u>My Utmost For His Highest</u> *(Oswald Chambers, Dodd, Mead and Company, ©1935) and the devotion started with* **John 14:31** *"Arise, let us go hence." But I'm so afraid! I'm afraid of making a mistake. I'm afraid of making the wrong decision. How can I know? God, you know I want more than anything to do your will and hear you say, "Well done." I want to stand on my decision with God-given conviction. Give me direction, Lord! I need you to show me clearly!!...*

PRAISE!! I wrote down all the pros and cons of each option I have for the summer and Wisconsin was so obvious as the best choice. It's exactly what I've always wanted to do - build up kids' self-esteem and work with special needs kids.

A quote from chapel today: 'The word "Christian" means different things to different people...if we get our information from the Biblical material, there is no doubt that the Christian life is a dancing, leaping, daring life.'   EUGENE PETERSON

What an incredible statement, huh? I'm so high on my tiptoes I might fall over! I have peace about the decision to go to Wisconsin. Now I just await word from the camp - if God doesn't want me there, He could give them a reason to say no."

Camp Algonquin hired me as a camp counselor for elementary and middle school special needs girls. I loved working with them! I can say "loved" because I do not mind doing hard things if it seems that people will see Jesus in me by doing them. Helping a thirteen-year-old bathe herself and shave was humbling. My

THE JOY WEAVER - GRASSROOTS

heart hurt for her daily struggle to keep smooth and clean. Patience was practiced with our young drama specialist. She kept screaming as we walk-waded around an island in rock-infested waters. Marching to the craft cabin was a work of art with the kiddo in back. Only a dance or follow-the-leader game would coax her not to be tardy.

Campers stayed for a week of fun, culminating in The Bear Hunt. It was eerie. It was tense. Hopefully it wasn't torture! All the kids in all the cabins would dress warm and proceed to the shadowy trail after dark. If they braved the whole thing while hearing bushes crackle around snarly growls and grunts, they would win a bear patch. The Bear Hunt was the camp's big selling point. Their goal was to boost self-esteem, making kids proud of themselves for braving a dangerous bear.

As for maintaining my Christian witness, times were interesting. At the beginning of the camp season, I had asked about church on Sundays. Someone had responded dubiously, "It's a long way away, and no one goes." Since I didn't know anyone, and didn't have transportation, I resigned myself to that. I would slip away time to time to a small cabin that I used as a prayer chapel. I would play my Steven Curtis Chapman cassettes and sing along and pray. In a notebook, I kept camp stories, verses, and prayers, at least a few times a week. I needed that time alone with God to stay grounded and connected to Him.

I was so pleased when my girls began asking questions about God one night at bedtime. We were laying on our mattresses with the lights out after having trekked from the bathrooms 'neath the stars. I told them stories about my relationship with Jesus and explained how they could know God too. I planted seeds for another season. I prayed for numbers of campers by name long after my return to college.

Most of our staff were willing to talk religion. When we did, I targeted the topic of relationship with Jesus. My heart grew sick at one mocker's accusation, "What did Jesus Christ ever change? He died on a cross, and the world goes on." His unbelief shocked me; I felt like I had run into a brick wall. I was so taken aback that I failed to give an answer. Why had I remained silent when I knew so many vibrant testimonies of changed lives, including my own? For years that sad scene plagued me.

I met strong resistance, too, the night I challenged The Bear Hunt in our staff meeting. I wanted to know, "Why do we not tell the kids about the God who loves them and died to save them so their self-esteem will be based on the fact of love instead of fear-based fiction?" (Surely you realize that the bears were not real?) The staff must have all been mumbling because I don't recall their specific retorts.

The day we discussed evolution, I highlighted a complete dearth of intermediary specimens. Millions of halfwits in limbo would come forth from excavations all over the planet if creatures had morphed over millions of years! No one was mad.

Then came the bad language lesson. One counselor shared his philosophy that saying, "Oh fat!" (as I did) was no different than him saying "****!" Both were spoken harshly from the heart. I tucked that common sense into long term memory.

Colossians 4:6a *"Let your speech always be with grace..."*

Free from campers, we counselors went out on the town. Bars in the area were family-friendly pubs with menus, pool tables and darts. Without much experience in places like these, they seemed harmless enough to me. Being of age, I tried a few drinks without going overboard. We entertained ourselves in movie theaters, on horses, at the dock, in the lake, dancing in silly costumes or playing "Ha! Ha!" (Just try that – put your head on someone's stomach while they laugh, "Ha! Ha!")

Summer slipped by and things had been okay. Then a freakishly bad dream about Mom left me feeling motherless. I came out of my cabin running down the dirt path toward the main buildings. The crushing nightmare had ended vivid and red. I was sick to my stomach. I cried trying to find a phone not in use. When I finally heard her voice on the other end of the line, I could breathe again. She was fine!

In other hellish matters, my friend the youth pastor (not a camp role) had prodded me like Satan himself, "You know you're a wild child. Just let it out." Conversely, he sobbed for hours on the dock one night, expressing deep remorse for the consequences of irreversible choices. He was in pain, without the peace of Christ. It was an education in the raw tragedy of worldly living. I had rarely been exposed to it. And then…

I faced the test of a lifetime. A cute boy and I had been flirting off and on. I was unattached, and it had been three years since my last boyfriend. It was just goof off fun to me. But in the last couple days, as everyone cleaned, packed, and closed down the camp, I heard a rumor that sent chills down my spine. He wanted me. Sadly, I felt flattered. No one had ever desired me like that to my knowledge. It intrigued me!

That afternoon, alone in the bathroom stalls amid my chores, I sensed the Holy Spirit speak forcefully inside of me "Run!" I felt His urgency, His warning cry.

Oh, foolish girl! I reasoned, "How could I not hang out with everyone on the last night after a whole summer of camp?" We would all go to dinner, and play pool, and drink a little, and reminisce, and laugh. Pondering seemed harmless…

We all went out to wander the town. And he was clearly messing around. From camp to bar and bar to car, then to his room with others far. I was slipping down a slope of pleasurable curiosity. When the light went off, my world was crumbling.

BUT MY BEST FRIEND JESUS, King of Kings, Lord of Lords, Prince of Peace, Almighty God rose up righteously from His place in my spirit and *resisted with everything in Him in me*. He sounded an alarm in my conscience like a fire drill in hell. "What are you doing?! Stop! Get out of here!" Jesus was calling me away. Jesus persisted to preserve me. Finally, I obeyed. I said to the boy, "I'm sorry, I can't go through with this. I won't betray my best friend, Jesus." He heeded my decision and kindly sent me out. By God's grace I walked away. I was ashamed, and yet relieved.

2 Timothy 1:9-10 *"(God) has saved us, and called us with a holy calling, not according to our works, but according to His own purpose and grace which was granted us in Christ Jesus from all eternity, but now has been revealed by the appearing of our Savior Christ Jesus, who abolished death and brought life and immortality to light through the gospel,"*

Romans 6:11 *"Even so consider yourselves to be dead to sin, but alive to God in Christ Jesus.*

Philippians 1:9-11 *"And this I pray, that your love may abound still more and more in real knowledge and all discernment, so that you may approve the things that are excellent, in order to be sincere and blameless until the day of Christ; having been filled with the fruit of righteousness which comes through Jesus Christ, to the glory and praise of God."*

37 PENITENCE AND IMPATIENCE

    Sifting out my sorrow from summer's end took sober weeks of conversations with godly friends and repetitive confession and repentance before the Lord. He was the One I had hurt the most. Condemnation had been breathing down my neck with familiar glee, and fear had been strangling my heart with a death grip. They were not holy messengers. I was so disappointed in myself and concerned for all those I had shared Christ with. What a conflicting message I had disseminated. I imagined the gossip lofted on the wake of our departures. "She did – oh, she *didn't*?!"

    True! There was certain solace in that stance. The Lord had stood up for me and won my heart again. But temptation had drawn me closer to the edge of complete failure than I had ever allowed before, and it terrified me. I wanted a husband to hold me and comfort me so badly. Please God. How long would I have to wait?

Aug 28, 1990 A thought from all-girl's chapel today: Concerning a husband, God always gives His very best to those who leave the choice up to Him!

    Psalm 55:16-18a *"As for me, I shall call upon God, and the Lord will save me. Evening and morning and at noon, I will complain and* murmur, and He will hear my voice. He will redeem my soul in peace from the battle which is against me."

Psalm 55:22 *"Cast your burden upon the Lord and He will sustain you; He will never allow the righteous to be shaken."*

<u>Sep 6, 1990</u> Put your arms around my husband today. Keep him strong and encouraged. I love him!

<u>Sep 7, 1990</u> *"He will send from heaven and save me; He reproaches him who tramples upon me. God will send forth His lovingkindness and His truth."* **Psalm 57:3**

<u>Sep 8, 1990</u> Help me to live, eat, and breathe You, Lord. Prepare me for my husband. I pray you would guide and protect him – make him love you with his whole heart.

The band leader had picked me up at the airport when I returned from Wisconsin. But I was ready to be done with Jared. Our listless connection and his get-together with yet another girl was more than I could take. I was struggling to be civil anymore. I acknowledged him as a brother in Christ and prayed for him. But I distanced myself in person with determined self-protection. Mom was fed up with his callous treatment of her daughter. Tired of on again – off again stories, she and Dad had grown anxious for me to meet God's man. They were praying earnestly!

All that to say, the praise band never reconvened. I chose to join a weekly prayer group instead.

<u>Sep 25, 1990</u> God, I don't know why but I feel achy inside. Maybe because three couples are getting married over Christmas

break; one is Carolyn, my former roommate. Sarah and Eric will be engaged over Christmas, and Tonya and James might be married this summer. Tammy and Steve are hanging tight through their separation while he's gone on an internship. And then there's me – and I feel like I'm going to go crazy so no one will want to marry me anyway. I feel like my past sins will maim my life as long as I'm on Earth. Will I ever be truly happy Lord?

On Sunday, the college group leader read an excerpt from A.W. Toser's book – *Knowing God* or *In Pursuit of God*? ...Toser says that You, Lord, are sufficient for every possible need we could have – emotionally, mentally, and spiritually.

Again Lord, I come down to life being a struggle. I'm doing all the right things and yet I feel bad inside, and I'm even scared to think of a real relationship with some guy. My track record isn't very good so far, you know? But I heard a good phrase on the radio last night – when one begins to worship, then he begins to grow.

Oct 1, 1990 Lord, I pray you would help me to be consistent in my prayer and Scripture reading. Help me not to become haughty or puffed up in it. Help me to learn new and fresh things every day – keep my love for You alive. Give me patience for the day I meet my husband and prepare me to be a godly wife.   Love, Nancy

Oct 3, 1990 I pray for my husband – help him grow and learn about You and love You with all his heart, mind, and soul.

Oct 10, 1990 I studied some and then got ready for Nita's wedding – it was a very nice wedding...Saw Kevin and Chrissy and their wedding pictures (from August).

On Sunday, **Bill**, Denise, Paula, and I went to church and college group. Then I came home to study and took a nap.

Nancy McComb

Nov 5, 1990 ...I also pray You would forgive me for carrying bitter feelings on Saturday night towards my friend for flirting. Help me to respond in love and maturity. Father, please help me to be above reproach in my relationships with male friends.

I can't identify "my friend" with certainty; but by this time, Bill McComb and I had bonded over the frustration of relationships. "I hate girls," he would smirk, as his attempts to find love had not worked out. "I hate guys" I would tease, because summer still felt bad, and the band had broken down. We were just kidding around. But would I ever find the right guy?

38 CHENANIAH CHEER

I had caught sight of the high school girl trying out for our Southwestern College music group, The Chenaniah Singers. (Chenaniah was the Chief of the Levites in charge of music and carrying the ark in 1 Chronicles 15:22, 27 & 26:29). The girl was beautiful, with long blond wavy curls and a confident air. I surmised she must be good to have been invited to try out during high school. I was a college senior, hoping to earn a spot in the PR tour group for a scholarship. I needed to pay for an extra fifth year of classes so I could finish up a hefty elementary teaching degree.

That old disturbing sense of "I'm not enough" was weighing on me again. I loathed having to compete for something I needed. Jealousy's twisted priorities threatened to wring my intestines with acute discomfort. Contentious thoughts were provoking fear and a lack of trust in God. What if I could not win a spot? How would I pay for school? God answered my worries with His Father's heart. I must reject this hellish response or succumb to a bad attitude of frustration and strong dislike of my perceived threat.

Jealousy and insecurity were old foes of mine. Battles with them had become apparent in middle school when the word "jealous" first appeared in my journal. One morning I had drawn a blank heart bordered with ink lace on the page. The middle was left empty so I could report on news of that night's church social. I was hoping the boy I liked would invite me to couple skate or ask me to be his girlfriend! When I got home that night, I wrote down all the facts.

Mar 20, 1982 It was a lot of fun. I got blisters which hurt quite a bit. I skated for about 5 hours…I never skated the couple skates. He did not ask me a single question. He went over and talked to *her* though. Shameful as it may be, I was jealous.

A few weeks later, I reflected on another event, having learned a bit better how to cope. Had Mom or Dad given me some good advice? Or maybe God had offered me some sense?

Apr 13-14, 1982…We were at church youth camp. He was there. Friday night was fun. Saturday was super. He and a friend took my slippers, and we all chased each other all afternoon. Then they got more boys and dragged me *and her* into the ocean in our clothes. It was fun. I'm not jealous about them taking *her* in, too, because she's my good friend and the Lord will give us each the perfect mate someday. So I'm not worried.

That experience had been my warmup. A more difficult trial was on its way. In seventh grade I had been the only girl in youth group! The guys and I would play flag football, tackle each other for fun, wrestle, or play keep away. I loved the comradery, goofing off with my male companions. I didn't mind being "just one of the guys." And then everything changed.

Pastor Jim and Shirley, Grand Pastor, and some of their affiliates, were called to lead another church in San Jose, California. A new pastor's family came, with a daughter two years younger, named Teresa. I was thrilled! And then I grew frustrated. "All" the boys were enamored with her. She also gained popularity with "all" the little kids, and families that needed a babysitter.

THE JOY WEAVER - GRASSROOTS

She and I grew to be close friends, but inwardly I ached with self-doubt. I felt second rate in our small church family where I had been firmly rooted for over five years. I had gladly welcomed her, and now it felt like I was losing out. Why was she permitted to accept a date to the Senior High Banquet while still in middle school? Kids her age weren't allowed to attend that event. I had waited until I was old enough, and still hadn't been asked to accompany anyone. Her mom, as pastor's wife, had let it happen.

Teresa's unfair advantage was painful to me. God's Word had taught me to come to Him. **1 Peter 5:7** *"...casting all your anxiety on Him, because He cares for you."* So I sure did complain to Jesus! He might agree with me that I was drawing the short end of the stick!

Talking to Him about my struggles helped me reason a little better, but it did not change the circumstances. Wrestling with insecurity and jealousy was arduous.

Another situation that had made me jealous at school was a classmate trying to get between me and Jenna. You already know how important Jenna's friendship was to me that first half of tenth grade. I strongly depended on her. I felt threatened if the other girl competed for Jenna's favor. I felt I had a lot to lose.

Sep 11, 1984 This morning Jenna called and said she was late, and her sister was bringing her to school. I was kind of disappointed, but figured I'd see her at school. She never came. It was a boring day without her. At break I was going to call her as soon as I went to the bathroom. As I was going to the bathroom, another girl came up to me and said, "I'm going to call Jenna. Want to come?"

I felt jealous and told her I'd just been going to call. We went up and I got in front of her (in line) so I could call. But she didn't want to wait and used the pay phone. At lunch I got out of class as fast as I could and got up to the phones because I wanted to be the first to call her. But no one answered the phone again this time.

At lunch, the other girl and I ate with our 7th graders, and she told me, "Jenna's not home yet." I said, "I know, I tried to call her." It's very tense between us. I think we're jealous of each other and each of us is trying to "fight" for Jenna. I feel so over-powered by her. She's known Jenna longer…I feel jealous. Jenna is the greatest friend I have ever had in my entire life…I feel so relaxed around her. She understands me ….We help each other out and encourage each other and talk about our walk with God. I think I'd die if our friendship ever ended.

As you know, Jenna left HBA by Christmas. Though there were new friends all around, at church and at school, I was always analyzing the social landscape for a place to belong without stress or insecurity. I wanted to be comfortable in my own skin without worrying about other people so much. Would that ever be possible? As a Christian, it seemed like it should be. In each new incident that caused me grief, I was casting my cares on Him. But I was a slow learner at figuring out how to be confident in Him.

Mar 19, 1985 Life is sure confusing…things are going all the wrong way. The guy I like flirts with another girl, maybe because he's known her for a long time, or maybe he does like her. I'm not saying I'm jealous of her – with the Lord's help I never want to be jealous of anyone. It's miserable being jealous and it just shows I'm not happy with how God made me, and I'm not trusting Him with my life.

At one point, Teresa's parents considered sending her to HBA and I was to host her for a visit. I knew she'd love it and was excited to show her around. But again, I was blindsided when the guy I liked showed interest in her and made remarks about the girls in my youth group. That feeling of being invaded and shoved aside hit me again. Maybe I wasn't going to be safe at school anymore?

Apr 10, 1985 At lunch I said I was bringing my friend from church to school and the boy I liked said, "Oh yeah?" Then to his guy friend, "You should see the girls in her youth group! I didn't think girls could be that pretty and go to Sunday School. I wonder what they do on their dates?" I was surprised when he said that and kind of jealous. I wonder if he thinks I'm pretty. Who knows. Ooooh! I'm so in love with him.

I'm really glad Teresa is coming to school with me – we're gonna have a BLAST! But I'm kind of...not really jealous, but sad and jealous mixed. I'll bet he thinks she's really pretty and gives her tons of attention and the other guys will too. I may end up getting ignored. I hope not. But she ALWAYS gets about any guy she wants. Guys always tell me...or someone she's with, that they think she's cute or pretty.

No one ever says anything about me – or at least not that I hear about. Such is life. I'd better quit talking about this because I'm feeling sorry for myself, and no one likes a pouter. The Lord will work everything out – IN HIS TIME!

Despite choosing to be optimistic about Teresa's visit, I wound up feeling miserable. The guy I liked, and another boy, indicated they would like to give her a ride home. But she was riding home with me after school to go to Wednesday Bible study.

Apr 17, 1985 He snapped his fingers sort of like, "shucks!" I felt so angry...He's got his car and I'm sure he would have been GLAD to give her a ride home – he lives right by her. The day got progressively worse...I was in such a gross mood that I acted super weird. Basketball practice was kind of yuck, too. I kept making fouls and not doing the right thing. As a family, we went to Pizza Hut, and I was in a lousy mood. I was wallowing in self-pity because I'm 16 and she's 14 and she always gets all (or most of) the guys. I feel like a real piece of trash! Well, I guess that's her good fortune. I can't be jealous because she's my li'l sis and I really do love her a lot.

Somehow, I always climbed out of the insecure pit back into a working friendship with her. Many more girls had joined us in youth group by now. One of the older ones confided in me that she was struggling with a sense of competition with Teresa. I sure knew how she felt! I divulged how hard it had been for me since the beginning, and that I understood her struggle. I also tried to share encouragement for dealing with things. Later, I wrote:

Apr 28, 1985 It took me a long time to get over being jealous of Teresa and disliking her. Thank the Lord she never really knew how much I disliked her sometimes. I still struggle, but I just keep trying to turn it over to the Lord and try to be my own person. Teresa has grown up and matured a lot, and I love her with all my heart now. She's my little sister. I told my struggling friend about my experiences and encouraged her not to worry about Teresa, but to just be herself because she has a great personality.

Fast forward past the girl coveting my high school boyfriend. Then pause to note my internal flare-ups if other girls attracted too much attention from my first best bud in college. Would these silent mean-girl insecurities ever stop bugging me? I needed help!

Psalm 119:11 says, *"Your word I have treasured in my heart, That I may not sin against You."*

In desperation I looked in the index of my Bible for verses about jealousy. Memorizing them would give me a "sword of the Spirit" to slay competitive thoughts and feelings. I was sick of being plagued by jealousy. I badly wanted some confident peace!

James 3:16-18 *"For where jealousy and selfish ambition exist, there is disorder and every evil thing. But the wisdom from above is first pure, then peaceable, gentle, reasonable, full of mercy and good fruits, unwavering, without hypocrisy. And the seed whose fruit is righteousness is sown in peace by those who make peace."*

This passage spun me 180 degrees in the opposite direction from jealousy. It taught me that the root of it was selfish ambition. This was my problem, not the other person's problem. And it told me where I could find something much better. Wisdom from above was pure, peaceful, gentle, reasonable, full of mercy and good fruit. Wow. Those sounded delectable! Next time I felt like my relationships, possessions or positions were encroached upon, I would quote those verses, and ask God to give me His wisdom from above. His truth would transform my sinful heart and mind.

Philippians 2:3-4 *"Do nothing from selfishness or empty conceit, but with humility of mind regard one another as more important than yourselves; do not merely look out for your own personal interests, but also for the interests of others."*

The next biggest threat to unravel my sense of security came three years later. Instead of flipping out when I caught sight of the younger girl auditioning for Chenaniah, I recited those verses to work on calming my inner turmoil. But this was hard for me. I was worried. What if that girl pushed me out of a chance to earn a vocalist scholarship? I felt like I had earned it. I was older. I had been singing in choir for four years... taken voice lessons... served on the praise band, built relationships with the other people trying out. And I needed that money for my last year of school. Hmm. That was sounding a lot like selfish ambition!

Could I trust the Lord to take care of me, regardless of who was chosen? Strengthened with the wisdom of those verses I had memorized, I yielded my head and heart to the power of the Holy Spirit. When doubts pelted my ponderings, I drew my "sword."

I also chose to apply God's wisdom: pure, gentle, and reasonable, full of mercy and good fruit. I could think about her life circumstances. What was her story? What did she need? I could empathize with the difficulty of auditioning as an outsider. I could rejoice with those who rejoice. If this young lady was talented enough to earn a spot, then she would be a blessing to the team.

This time, I had taken the victory! I had chosen to be a caring person, an outward thinker, a giver instead of a taker. By trading twinges of jealousy and enmity for truthful meditation and prayer for her, stinking thinking was disabled. In its place emerged a pathway for comradery and friendship.

Her name did not show up in my journal during tryouts. I had nothing to worry about anymore, and I was too busy to write. But she did show up in my writings that summer as we bonded during the Chenaniah tour. Yes! Both of us had been chosen!

One night on the trip, while settling into a host home, she was feeling lonely, still the new kid in the group. She came to me for encouragement, and I was glad to genuinely care, listen, and pray without a hint of competition or hypocrisy. How grateful to God I was for experiencing the beauty of His ways. Being selfless had rendered me kind, confident and secure in the Lord. Imagine that!

39 HOW DEEP IS YOUR LOVE

This first day of spring classes in January 1991, I was anxious. Waiting for a boy to declare his intentions was tough! For several years I had dedicated deep respect and unconditional love to three different guys, serving each as a loyal friend and constant companion, encouraged by the mutual appreciation. I would imagine us married and wait hopefully. My friends knew, my parents knew, while each guy probably did too. Yet eventually I'd realize he was looking elsewhere for romance. When my third dream vanished in mid-air, God had been hinting at the best yet!

Last fall, Bill McComb had begun to visit our apartment from time to time. He was friends with one of my roommates, so it made perfect sense. He would sit in our front doorway since the Student Handbook forbade him to come in. And thus, our jokes began about hating girls and hating guys. It wasn't true, of course. But both of us had suffered at the hand of relationships, or the lack thereof. So we would goof around about it and laugh heart to heart to console ourselves.

We had been crossing paths for a good while now. There was that day he had invited me to church last spring. Then he had joined the praise band, and we had appreciated riding together. Young Life ministry staff had recruited both of us to serve with teens. And this year we were each working in student government with the Blue Fellowship group. It was now our responsibility to plan the Fall Festival.

His brave heart was tender the November night he asked me, "Since we're both Blue Fellowship leaders, I'm going and you're going. Would you just want to go together?" "Sure!" I smiled. There on the steps of the student center, he leaned in and gave me a brief eskimo kiss – soft swishes nose to nose. Maybe it was no big deal… kind of brotherly? Our conversations were lingering.

When my car refused to start, leaving me repeatedly stranded in the early part of December, it was Bill to the rescue several times. It dawned on me that our interactions were illuminating a plausible attraction to each other. "Life has taken an interesting turn as Bill seems to be interested in me. He wrote me a very nice encouraging note yesterday."

Simultaneously, an HBA friend and I had been writing off and on since graduation, lately with increasing frequency. I had grown curious if anything would develop when I went back to Hawaii for Christmas break. I felt wary of two-timing potentially interested parties; but neither had made any declaration of intention. Since I had read into things during past deep friendships, I would just have to wait and see.

A few days before everyone left for winter vacation and the holidays, Bill invited me out. "I went to 'The Messiah' with Bill last night, and then we came back to campus and had pizza. We studied in the lounge until 1 AM. I had a good time with him, but I'm still being cautious. It's progressing carefully, as it should be."

My first day back home in Hawaii, "Before I left, Bill brought me a birthday card with scratch-n-sniff roses, and we said good-bye. He gave me wallets and a 5x7 of our group Christmas picture. It turned out nice. We hugged good-bye and before I took off, he sent me a teddy bear via Tammy. I like Bill a lot. I keep thinking about him. I'm still wondering about my other friend, Lord. Give me wisdom/discernment. Mom told me tonight that she's praying I at least meet my husband this year."

When Mom and Dad picked me up from the airport, I had talked non-stop about Bill McComb during the ride home. He had the sweetest disposition, while being handsomely sporty, rugged, and manly. And he had so many desirable qualities! He could sing, loved kids, liked to be on time, was clean and organized. He worked hard, got along with everyone, and played volleyball and basketball. He served in leadership and was paying his own way through college – displaying excellent responsibility and independence for one so young. He was serious about his faith, and he was super funny. That was just the beginning of what I knew about him!

The question mark in Hawaii gently faded, though we did hit the beach one afternoon for fun. A fact I had never known about my friend there was that he did not want kids! Whoops. That was a clear line in the sand for me! Besides, he never proposed our friendship transform into anything else, so I was freed up to pursue Bill wholeheartedly. "I bought Bill a Maui Surf Club Gecko t-shirt from Crazy Shirts. It will match his fluorescent pink shorts. I wish I could give it to him now. I still miss him. Today I thought about how conscientious he is and yesterday how our standards match up so far. I feel myself starting to cling to him emotionally."

Bill was missing me too. He wrote me a letter on Christmas Day from his mom's house in Park City, UT. It was postmarked December 27. I was ecstatic a few days later to see his handwriting on an envelope in my mailbox! I wrote him back after a frustrating movie night, expressing conservative convictions about sizzling scenes. Other news went on page after page. I glued them together and creased them like an accordion, sandwiched between two post cards of Hawaii. This was getting fun.

Nancy McComb

Bill would fly back to Phoenix ahead of me, so we planned over the phone for him to pick me up at Sky Harbor Airport in my car. I mailed him the key. Dad said that if Bill detailed the Colt, I would know *he* was the one! After touching down in The Valley of the Sun, Bill met me warmly at my gate. Reciprocal affection sparkled amid bashful interactions. As we went to baggage claim for my luggage, I realized his new earring sparkled too. He took me to lunch at Denny's where I covered my mouth as I ate. I was extra nervous and self-conscious now. *My car was spotless*!

Back on campus, days before school started, we settled into our apartments, ran errands for gas, cash, groceries, school supplies, etc. and hung out with friends. Our crew watched movies during open dorms. Eric and Sarah had been separated last semester, due to Eric's ministry internship. They were gladly catching up face to face. Bill and I were spending tons of time together as we had more and more to talk about. And sometimes we were affectionate, like a hand on a shoulder as we all hung out together. Yet he was not showing any signs of making us official.

So here we were moving a bit fast, too fast for my liking, without a declaration of commitment. I was getting anxious, even aggravated. I knew I would not survive long in another ambiguous affiliation! I believed it was the man's job to lead the woman. So I kept waiting to hear something from him. I wanted clarity or space!

Unbeknownst to me, Bill had made his own earnest plea with God. After all the discouraging attempts to get together with girls, Bill had told the Lord that when the right girl finally came along, *she* would have to be the one to say something!

So here we were then, the first day of classes in the spring of 1991. I could not take it anymore! When I saw Bill that afternoon, I said to him, "I need to talk to you." And he agreed. First, we had supper and went for a jog. I was nervous. I felt tense.

THE JOY WEAVER - GRASSROOTS

He was nervous, and he felt tense, too! He had grown discouraged in defining the relationship with other girls. Bill's mind was mulling it over. What would it be *this* time? 1) She doesn't like me and doesn't want to spend time together. 2) She likes me, but just wants to be friends. 3) She likes me and wants something more.

We returned to the picnic table outside my apartment. It was already dark, so stars were shining in the crispy night sky. He was waiting for me to say something since I had initiated this conversation. We both stepped up on the picnic bench and laid back on the stone table, shoulders barely touching, faces staring into the heavens, both seemingly holding our breath. Palm fronds high above us were flapping in the breeze. For a bit, we were silent. Then I inhaled nervously and sighed, "It's good."

Then he sighed, too. I told him I really liked him. I had enjoyed the ways our friendship had been growing. But I needed to know where we were heading – did he have a plan? We had become nearly inseparable lately. If being a couple was not on the agenda, then I needed space. At that point, he jumped in to affirm his feelings for me and we chatted for a while, relishing our journey. Neither of us wanted to quit.

The weeknight curfew was 8PM, so our watches insisted we finish up and go in. We sauntered to the entry of my apartment, while I was still waiting for a concrete declaration. I asked timidly, "So…what's the verdict? Are we a couple? Are we dating?" He peered at me simply satisfied, smiling, "I guess we're dating!" I chicken-pecked him and ducked inside our doorway dazzled. Was I dreaming? My roommates were inside to celebrate with me as I threw myself onto the couch.

Later that evening, as I reached for the shower knob, I searched for God's reaction. He didn't speak, but I sensed His presence. It felt like He was smiling. I was facing another blank canvas with a lot of questions, but He was with me, and I had peace. Bill McComb was a really great guy!

Behold! **Monday** January 21, 1991 was exactly 52 weeks, 1 year, since the day I had journaled last January 22, 1990. It was on a Monday I had written about my hopeful expectation of a perfect-for-me man, like God had provided a perfect-for-me job and a perfect-for-me car. What a miracle – exactly one year to the day!

Yet I was unaware of it. God's Sovereignty, so precisely displayed, would remain a hidden treasure for over thirty years, to be unearthed in the writing of this book!

I would sooner come to realize that God had answered my earnest plea of the summer after high school. I had asked Him to let me be friends with my future husband at least a year before knowing we'd get married.

But even that revelation could wait a little bit. Tonight, on this starry-eyed stage, I was not projecting "husband." I was finally relishing, "my very own boyfriend!" And soon enough, God's plan was going to prove itself wonderful!

40 IT'S OFFICIAL!

On Friday September 20, 1991, Bill and I were sitting on the dusty conference table in the same seat prints we had made the day before. The second story of the student center had not yet been completed, so cement floors and exterior walls with big windows looked like one of those Big City, industrial-sized, pricey, modern apartments. We had watched funny scenes of students passing by below and then prayed together about his dad and my parents coming for the weekend. It was nice.

While my parents already knew that we were planning to get married, the official hoops to jump through were still before us. They had never even met him!

Sep 20, 1991 Mom and Dad got into town about 5:30. They called to say they'd meet us in ½ hour. They were late and showed up when I had run into the house, so Bill met them on his own. It all seemed so natural. We drove to Olive Garden and waited ½ hour. Mom and I talked on the bench while Dad and Bill talked standing up. I asked Mom, "So what do you think?" and she said, "Oh, he's a doll!"

Dinner was great – Bill paid. He told his testimony; and we talked about mission opportunities. Mom asked him to tell his life story, so he did. I learned new things!

We came back and went over to their apartment at Sierra Grande which was very nice and beside the pool. We showed Bill the video of John and I singing two songs – John singing the song he had written. Mom had brought the ring section from the Best catalogue and we looked through there.

The next day Bill and I were busy preparing for my dad's birthday dinner. Bill Sr. would be coming as well, so our parents would have a chance to become acquainted. The best part was, Bill and I had come up with a plan for the big ask. We had chosen together to become an official dating couple eight months ago. Together, we had come up with a funny way for Bill to ask Dad's permission to get engaged.

Sep 21, 1991 The party was great. We sat around while Dad got rolls and Bill got lemonade and the casserole warmed. We hadn't been eating long when Bill's dad was back early (he'd stopped in ahead to say he'd be late). We had a wonderful time.

Dad opened his presents, and we made a big deal about the card being saved for last and him needing to read it left side before right side, without peeking ahead. There was my note on the left, followed by, "P.S. 'Oh please, oh please!'" and Bill's note on the right, followed by, "P.S. 'Can I marry your daughter?'" It went over well and when we'd finished laughing – Bill officially asked my dad in person (with his dad there, too!). My dad said yes with a little speech about me and what Bill had done for me. Then Bill's dad gave a speech about me impacting Bill's life. It was wonderful and memorable.

The sweet words I will never forget are when Dad told Bill, "We knew you were the one, because when Nancy called to tell us about you, she had answers instead of questions." Yes! Every longing of my heart made perfect sense now. What a gift!

THE JOY WEAVER - GRASSROOTS

Bill proposed to me on November 17, 1991. We had been to church that morning and then eaten spaghetti lunch on the same picnic table where we had had "the talk" back in January. We had planned to hike Squaw Peak seven miles away but decided on Cholla Mountain near campus. He had his Bible with him, and he was acting funny. On top of the mountain, we sat down. And he began to give a speech.

You know our life verse is Psalm 48:14, "For such is God, our God forever and ever; He will guide us until death." If we believe that, we must be re-evaluating all the time and making sure that God is at the center of things...So I've been evaluating our relationship and reading, and I found this verse, "The man said, 'This is now bone of my bones, And flesh of my flesh; She shall be called Woman, Because she was taken out of Man. For this reason a man shall leave his father and his mother, and be joined to his wife; and they shall become one flesh." (Genesis 2:23-24)

I had gotten chills realizing that he was proposing. I looked at him with a smile on my face and he grabbed my hands and said, "Nancy Lynn...I'm asking you to be my lawfully wedded wife." He put the engagement ring on my finger. We hugged and it was really neat. I was excited – but more calm because it all seemed so natural. We prayed together asking for God's blessing on our preparations and relationship and asked for help in keeping us pure. Then we sang songs, *One God* and *Seek Ye First*, and talked about plans a little.

After a while he said, "Time to go, my butt's getting sore." I love him so much! At one point I had hugged him and looked him in the eyes and said, "I always wanted to marry my best friend, and you are my best friend!" He answered, "You're my best friend, too." He gave me a bookmark last night as a memoir that says, "Happiness is being married to your best friend." It has the date on the back and a message.

Next day, we announced our engagement in chapel. We had already decided some days ago that the best wedding date would be May 9th. So now it was official!

41 AND SO IT BEGINS

I adore carnival rides and roller coasters and amusement park thrills of all kinds. That feeling of excitement when you are strapped in and know that the adventure is going to be fun and scary and take your breath away and then give it right back so you can whoop and holler with delight…YES! I'm never half in or out about getting in line for one of those, and my enjoyment of it usually absorbs any fear factor.

William McComb had spun my world around within weeks of realizing we cared for each other deeply. We dated eleven months and were engaged for six. Bill's charm and humor with decisive maturity were a breath of fresh air! From beginning to beginning, we marveled at God's providence in every detail of our two lives becoming one - even before we were born! God had maneuvered plans for us as Everlasting Father, Wonderful Counselor and Prince of Peace. He was present in every way we longed for Him. And He never charged us a penny for serving as our miracle matchmaker, life coach, wedding planner and travel agent!

BEFORE WE WERE BORN

Bill's mom and dad were also named Bill and Nancy! They had gone separate ways and both remarried. We would be the new

Nancy McComb

Bill and Nancy McComb. Neither of us saw this as coincidence. God had written our love story even before The Creation.

BEFORE WE MET

Our childhoods had many similarities. We were both taught to respect and obey our parents and were spanked when naughty. Both sets of parents had served their communities, attended church, and hosted big social events. Bill's parents had been integral in early stages of Park City development. His mom had helped form a sister city relationship with Courchevel, France. My parents had served in missions, being used of God to transform individuals and communities with the gospel

Both clans honored extended family, generation to generation. We were often surrounded by aunts, uncles, cousins, grandparents, and great grandparents. We had happy memories of long road trips, with us kids riding unbuckled, playing games on platforms over luggage. We had both been in Central America.

Christmas mornings had sparkled with surprises from creative parents. My parents planned elaborate scavenger hunts, and Bill's parents hid the fun underneath big bedsheets. Birthdays were a party around the table. My brother or I would find a heap of presents at breakfast when we woke up. At Bill's house, even siblings received a goodie of some sort at their place setting.

Both of us had committed ourselves to the Lord and guarded full physical intimacy as a gift to enjoy in lifelong marriage. As we exchanged stories, Bill told me unapologetically that if I had slept with the boy at Camp Algonquin, he would not be dating me. Since God had kept him pure as an unbeliever; he expected that his Christian wife would have saved herself, too.

THE JOY WEAVER - GRASSROOTS

BEFORE DATING

One day, months after becoming Bill's girlfriend, I perceived a series of memories playing one by one in my mind, as if flipping pages backwards in a picture book. I saw myself watching Bill at unique times all year, curious about him, his life, and relationships, especially ones I was not a part of. Those flashbacks astounded me! I was so "present" in those scenes. Yet somehow, very uncharacteristically, I had not consciously retained them nor written anything about them in my journals! God displayed proof of His miracle in living color, "See! All that time you had no idea!"

AS WE DATED

We were so right for each other! We ate our meals together on the picnic tables, studied for straight A's in the Student Center, took turns with one car and two bank accounts, and asked God for help to lead us in all of our new planning. We learned to "fight" as we exchanged values, beliefs, and brainstorms in uncomfortable conflicts, took turns getting what we wanted, or had fun wanting the same things. It was uncanny how often our clothes matched. We have some fun pictures from enjoying the coincidences!

ENGAGEMENT JITTERS

After we got engaged, the speed of our plans increased dramatically. This was adulting on a whole new level! We had so many decisions to make about jobs, housing, figuring out availability of extended family for the wedding, and budgeting for our future. If we married next summer, was beginning or end better? Could we swing an early May wedding date?

One concern was Bill's need for a job. We lived in separate on-campus housing, and I had been footing our basic bills that fall as Bill recuperated from hernia surgery. He had agreed to cover our basic living expenses in the spring, while I was student teaching.

Though spring was two months away, I grew anxious about flippant conversations and choices. He was healed up enough to host and play in a two-man volleyball tournament, but a new job was nowhere in sight. I spun the ring on my finger and called home.

It was just over a week since he had proposed. I knocked on his door after curfew and asked to talk with him outside. We discussed a lot of related topics back and forth until after 2AM. Then Bill went back to bed with the ring in his pocket. I needed to know he would take good care of me. He wanted to show that he would.

Bill set up an appointment with our Youth Ministry Professor, Tim Reed, the next morning. We met with him for an hour and a half and discussed work schedules, setting goals, attitudes about marriage, and things we wanted the other person to work on. We wondered about slowing things down, and pushing back our wedding date, even a whole year until Bill finished college. Mr. Reed said he thought we could be ready either way. But he suggested we hold off on locking it down until fall classes were over and we had talked with our families over Christmas break.

Bill called about a new job opportunity that very day and was soon cleaning office buildings and churches for a man at Palmcroft, who owned his own business. The earnestness and speed with which Bill responded gave me all the assurance I needed. Since I had returned the ring, we devised a plan to keep our disengagement on the down low. The ring was loose, so we dropped it off to get resized. By the time the jeweler finished, we were wholehearted about being engaged and moving forward.

FULL SPEED AHEAD

Mom and Dad offered to buy our plane tickets to Hawaii for Christmas break in exchange for painting the house. That sounded like a great deal to us! Bill hung out with my brother for

THE JOY WEAVER - GRASSROOTS

the first time, and I showed Bill all the places I had grown up since third grade. He was also able to meet my church and HBA friends.

At that point in time, Mom was working for an OBGYN, Dr. Fong, a member of our church. I took care of my premarital appointment while home for Christmas. And Pastor Dick at International Baptist Church gladly hosted Bill and I for four premarital counseling sessions. We learned a lot about each other!

We also filled out paperwork for our marriage license and then picked it up downtown. With all the puzzle pieces falling into place, we were confident about a May 9 wedding date.

A BLESSED BUDGET

Our 1 in 10 happy marriage[16] was celebrated with a ceremony that cost $2000. Mom and Dad made three sacrificial installments each during the months of our engagement. With their generous funds, Bill and I were free to dream, plan and execute a day to remember! We did not take a single cent for granted. We felt blessed and enjoyed the challenge of working within the budget.

STARTING OFF

Mom handed us our first check for $150 at the end of December. I went with a girl friend to a wedding paper goods store and spent big money on trifold invitations with embossed white roses on black stripes. Over the next month, I bought matching programs, a wedding planning book, soundtracks for the special numbers, and sheet music. Bill and I perused the pages of the wedding planner book and began composing a program we both liked. Then we needed to know *where* to hold our wedding before continuing.

THE PLACE

We had been attending and serving in youth ministry, with Steve and Tammy from school, at Palmcroft Baptist Church. It was a large auditorium, and we only needed space for 150 guests. A hefty fee was involved for using the premises, so we reached out to my first college church, North Mountain Baptist. Bill's buddy, Brian Ellsworth, and his wife, Jo, were serving there, as newlyweds themselves. So, Brian and Bill made the arrangements. It was close to Southwestern College, attractive and traditional. The charge for use of the sanctuary and reception hall was $80.

THE DRESSES

Paula's mom was a seamstress and offered to sew my bridesmaid's dresses. I was honored and elated by such a lavish gift. I chose a simple pattern with two colors. The short-sleeved bust section was black, with a couple inches of robust black lace extending over the color change to teal. These business-smart, tea-length dresses clasped shut with jeweled black buttons. Black hats, ribbed nylons, and pumps completed the ensemble. As for a wedding dress, I found two styles of beautiful, fitted gowns at an outlet store for $200 each. But no matter how I organized budget cuts, I could not strategize squeezing one in.

It was an act of God the day I walked into my apartment discussing wedding gown options. My freshman roommate, shorter and seemingly more petite than me, said, "I have a wedding dress that I never used! I was engaged, but we broke it off. What size are you?" We measured our wrists, busts, and waists and found we were near the same size! She had never altered the dress, so it would still be long enough for me to wear.

My only problem was that it hung off the shoulders. Otherwise, it was gorgeous, better than anything I could have imagined! The exquisite dress, headdress, and veil were designed in a style I deeply appreciated. It had cost Laticia the same as half of our wedding budget! She was happy to share it if I did not permanently restructure it, and returned it dry cleaned afterward. I wouldn't need one hanging in my closet anyway.

MATERIAL SOLUTIONS

The day Paula and I went to look for dress material and accessories, JoAnn Fabrics "just so happened" to be having a 40% off sale! We found material, supplies, white tulle, and a large lace insert. Paula's mom, Elsie, would use the tulle and insert to make an add-on for my dress that would cover chest, back, and shoulders. She even hand-sewed hundreds of pearly white beads and iridescent sequins on it so it would tie in with the gown! The whole upper section, which buttoned in back, was tacked gently into the bust of the garment and would easily detach later, without harming the original masterpiece. Her workmanship was exquisite!

A DATE TO WEDDING SHOP

Bill and I went to Paradise Valley Mall. We found white pumps at the Payless shoe store for $10. Our friend Marissa, who worked in one of the fancier department stores, used her 33% employee discount to help me buy my fancy earrings for $6. We pre-paid Bill's $80 tuxedo rental and looked for snazzy groomsmen's gifts at *Things Remembered*. We found a perfect gift for Bill's dad, his best man. It was an emerald felt golf green on an oak slab with an engraved plaque that read, "You're the best dad in the 'hole' world!" Bill's dad was an avid golfer, so we loved the humor of the desk organizer with signatures and wedding date etched in.

THE PHOTOGRAPHER

Trudy recommended the professional photographer from her and Nate's wedding. Mimi Hershey gave us line-item discounts for a total cost of $750! Her kindness was a relief with our exact resources. On wedding day, she was playful and funny. We kept laughing as she gave us instructions, where to go and what to do. Classy albums and photographs were shipped to us weeks later, after many rolls of film had been developed. Digital photography was an emerging field, not yet available for practical application.

THE WEDDING CAKE

A friend of a friend at church agreed to make our wedding cake for $150. I flew in the face of long-standing tradition when I chose to trim the white frosted layers with a black icing shell design. The crisp contrast would coordinate with our teal, black and white wedding. The informal arrangement ended up causing great concern as the wedding approached. I had trouble connecting with her as she had never sent confirmation or billed me ahead. Days before the wedding, we finally talked on the phone. She fulfilled her part of the bargain in the nick of time and rushed the cake into the reception hall not long before we headed down the aisle!

THE FLOWERS

I can thank The Yellow Pages for presenting me with a florist. My journal says it took the ladies and I two long hours to create a contract with affordable options, unlike the ones in my flowery imagination. I settled on choices less fancy than I had hoped. But all the key people would be beautified appropriately, and there was greenery for the candelabras. That invoice totaled another $150. I supplemented the large arrangements on stage with vases of silk flowers bought at MacFrugal's for $49.

FINISHING UP

As the checks arrived from Mom and Dad, we would cover the next items on our list. There were stamps for the invitations, gifts for the girls, gift wrap and bows, bows for the pews, rented items to put on stage, our fancy unity candle, nuts and mints for the cake and punch reception, tablecloths, and table wear, etc. One of my favorite orders was our crystal-clear Precious Moments cake topper, and the cake server set and crystal goblets, with our names and wedding date etched on them.

PERFECT TIMING

By wedding weekend, we were ready! I had graduated that Monday from five years of college with a bachelor's in Elementary Education. God had already given me a third-grade teaching job at Desert Cove Elementary, where I had student taught. Bill and I had been hired for the summer by FBC San Jose as day camp counselors. My parents had flown in for graduation, so they were around to help with the final preparations. And the rest of our families had flown in, even my mom's mom from Florida at the very last minute. She had originally said she could not come.

REHEARSAL WITH THE INLAWS

Bill's dad hosted our BBQ picnic rehearsal dinner on Friday night in the college cafeteria. Bill's mom, Nancy, and her husband Mike, his siblings Colin, Babbie, and Gavin, had arrived. It was my first chance to meet them. "Mom," as I called her early on, invited us to Park City, UT to celebrate a double 21st birthday for Bill and his twin, Scott. I would get to see Bill's hometown! Thankfully, the gathering lined up with the end of our four-week honeymoon trip, and we'd be passing right near there.

THE BIG DAY

Bill stayed up the night before we got married, drawing me a poster-sized replica of the Psalm 18:2 fortress in God's hand. He had originally drawn it on a small piece of paper during his first ever mission trip flight to Japan. How I loved that man's heart, tenderly leading and giving, setting God as the head of our home.

Nancy McComb

I had fallen asleep on the couch after packing up my apartment, tossing and turning with excitement, "We're getting married tomorrow!" Our big day was also everyone's last window to check out of on-campus housing. It started off as a crazy morning!

Bill and the groomsmen were up and out early, taking things to storage. They used my car since my roommates and family could give me rides. Then the landline in my apartment rang (the only kind of phone we had in those days). One of my car's tires had gone flat! That caused some drama, though not insurmountable. We had been warned, by those married before us, to expect things to go wrong on wedding day. Bill put on a spare tire until John or Colin, not in the wedding party, would have time to go and get it fixed. Later, someone dropped it off at our hotel.

Mom and Dad helped haul my stuff to storage before we headed to the church. The clock was ticking! When I think back now, it was one big happy party. Girls were in one side of the church putting on makeup and curling hair. Guys were on the other side dressing up and who knows? I wasn't there!

Mom was concerned about the no-show wedding cake. For good reason! She was finally glad to pass on the check I had scribbled hurriedly for the cake lady. Meanwhile, one of the girls was adding last minute curls to my fading perm.

With happy grins, big hugs, a gentle kiss, and not a lot to say, Bill and I saw each other alone before joining everyone for photographs. By the time we all met Mimi in the sanctuary, stomachs were growling. I had no lunch plan. And most skimped breakfast.

Somebody went for McDonald's cheeseburgers. Taking dramatically careful bites, and chewing fast between poses, added to the hilarity of our desperate cravings. I could just imagine dropping ketchup or mustard on my pure white garment. Thankfully, we all avoided disaster. And Mrs. Hershey was a great sport!

My roommate Laticia welcomed guests in the lobby. She showed them where to sign the guestbook and put their cards and gifts. My brother, John, and Bill's brother, Colin, ushered 130+/- guests into the long wooden pews on either side.

BECOMING MR. AND MRS.

My mom and Bill's mom lit the candles on stage. MaryLou and Vickie played *Fairest Lord Jesus* and *Jesu Joy of Man's Desiring* as attendants went forward: Bill's dad – Best Man, Paula – Maid of Honor, Eric and Sarah, Nate and Tonya, Andy and Tammy.

Dad and I stood arm in arm on this once-in-a-lifetime occasion, ready to enter the sanctuary. He would soon give me away to Bill for good. *The Bridal Chorus* swirled into the rafters, and we began to make our formal entrance.

One of the youth pastors we served with at Palmcroft had offered to do a wedding video. Having positioned himself in the back corner of the church, he was ready... until everyone stood for the bride. Well, *you* get the picture! We didn't complain about our free recording. The live feed was a wonderful memento.

I was thinking about Dad as we promenaded down the aisle: his strong godly character and patience with me through the years. Grandpa Joe and Bill met Dad and I in front. Then everyone opened hymnbooks to sing *When Morning Gilds the Skies*.

When morning gilds the skies, My heart awakening cries:
May Jesus Christ be praised;
Alike at work and prayer...to Jesus I repair...
May Jesus Christ be praised.
In heaven's eternal bliss The loveliest strain is this:

Nancy McComb

May Jesus Christ be praised;
The powers of darkness fear…When this sweet chant they hear;
May Jesus Christ be praised.
Be this, while life is mine, My canticle divine,
May Jesus Christ be praised;
Be this th' eternal song…Thro' all the ages on…
May Jesus Christ be praised.[17]

Grandpa Joe turned the service over to Dad, after Dad had given me to Bill with the traditional phrase, "Her mother and I do."

Randi and Danny sang two specials: *Our Love in Christ* and *Cherish the Treasure*. Dad gave the charge (or challenge) to Bill and me about the covenant of marriage and the seriousness of our commitment to each other. After prayer and traditional wedding vows, Bill read Genesis 2:23-24 to me, and I read Ruth 1:16-17 to him.

At that point we ran into a little trouble. Danny was singing *Perfect Union* as we went to light the unity candle. Funny thing though, having been warned to pre-light wicks to make them light faster later, we hadn't realized this one had basically disappeared! We joined our candles in the middle to light the unity candle, but it would not light! I panicked at first but then dug my thumbnail around its base to expose another section. As the singular flame rose, I sighed with relief – a "perfect union" spared!

THE RECEPTION

Our after-party was in the Wiley Center: embracing family, grabbing candid photos with friends, drinking sparkling punch and smashing cake in each other's faces. Then cake, mints, nuts, and punch for all. Our dads made speeches, gave toasts, as did others.

Bill removed my garter to fling at the single guys. I threw my bouquet for the single girls. Tradition! I chatted with my junior high girls from church. I felt so honored they had come!

Finally, it was time to be off! It felt rude to leave visiting relatives behind us. Thankfully, we would see them the next morning while opening gifts. Balloons and rice in hand, the guests exited to the parking lot. Church friends, Sheri and Starr, had just arrived from a baby shower. They were reunited with their husbands, Dave and Doug, just in time to join the parading send-off.

THE RIDE

Remember the amusement park rides? The key to enjoying them is to buckle in, sit back and relax, breathe deep, imagine the course, trust the architect and builder, and look forward to the thrill of it all, ups and downs!

We drove away from church that day in a Rolls Royce (thanks to Bill's dad), wearing royally fine clothes, with family and friends waving and cheering us on. Our celebration of marriage had only just begun! Newly declared "Mr. and Mrs.," riding toward the hotel was surreal. As our chauffeur swung tight around the narrow curve of elevated freeway where I-17 south turns onto I-10 east, I was in awe of all God had done, and I was glorying in the man beside me. We "soared" above the world below toward downtown Phoenix, on a level with the South Mountain horizon just miles away. I knew in that moment, with utter certainty, that this new holy matrimony, was the first day of the rest of our lives!

THE HONEYMOON

Thanks to our credit card reward points, we had booked two nights at the DoubleTree Resort and Hotel downtown. Bill carried me across the threshold in my froufrou wedding dress as I giggled. Then the newness of sharing space made me nervous. "Do you care which way the toilet paper rolls out? Do you squeeze your toothpaste on top or on bottom? Where would you prefer I put my stuff on the counter? Do you want to watch TV?" There would be many more questions where those ones came from!

Sunday morning, we drove to the Sierra Grande apartments, where my parents were staying next to Southwestern College. All our closest friends and family had come to join us. We had brunch, talked, laughed, and opened gifts. Sad news came that my Great Grandpa had gone to be with Jesus. He was celebrating that day, too. After saying good-bye to everyone, we left for a chill day to make our own plans, whatever and however we wanted.

We opened our pile of wedding cards at the hotel. Besides encouraging words, our loved ones had given us enough money to cover our honeymoon travel! We stayed a week at Uncle Ted's and Aunt Carole's cabin in Flagstaff, enjoying a trip to the Grand Canyon with Eric and Sarah. Then we hit the road for another three weeks: to James' and Tonya's wedding in Albuquerque, New Mexico; to John's graduation at the Air Force Academy in Colorado Springs with Mom and Dad; and then to Bill's and Scott's 21st birthday gathering with his family in Park City, Utah.

Home again in Phoenix, everything was in storage. We slept on the hide-a-bed couch at Nathan's and Trudy's apartment and enjoyed the comradery of their marriage advice. Some days later it was time to leave for San Jose. Bill (and I too, now) would work as summer day camp counselors at "the church on the hill" (First Baptist). Our very first newlywed home would be with the Quigleys, a sweet elderly couple who had housed Bill the last summer when he was interning.

READY TO SERVE

One of our new favorite songs in the car was sung by Gaither Vocal Band on their recently debuted album, *A Few Good Men*. The words of the chorus went like this:

THE JOY WEAVER - GRASSROOTS

Beyond the open door is a new and fresh anointing,
Hear the Spirit calling you to go.
Walk on through the door for the Lord will go before You
Into a greater power you've never known before.[18]

Our love for Jesus, worshiping together, working with kids, and travelling was an excellent gift bundle from God. We were young and flexible, serving in a great home church, surrounded by friends and family. Our relationship had been one big answer to prayer so far. We felt so ready for whatever was in front of us.

Gladly, we were clueless! If we'd seen God's agenda then and there, we may have wished to turn back before beginning. We had no idea of the impending number of faith-challenging, and sometimes death-defying journeys awaiting us up ahead. We just knew we wanted to serve God in full-time ministry. So we eagerly prayed for God to open doors.

Psalm 48:14 *"For such is God, Our God forever and ever; He will guide us until death."*

GLOSSARY

akamai	smart
bolsa	bag or purse
burro	a donkey
hale	house
haole	Caucasian
hapa	interracial Caucasian and Asian
kahuna	chief
kama'aina	island-born or permanent resident
kane	men
keiki	child
lanai	front porch
leeward	situated on the side sheltered from wind
lei	flower necklace in many varieties
lomi-lomi	chopped up mix
mahalo nui loa	thank you very much
mahalo	thank you
malihini	foreigner, newcomer
manzana	apple
Maui Gold	marijuana
mele kalikimaka	Merry Christmas
muumuu	a floor-length straight dress
ohana	family
pakalolo	marijuana
piña	pineapple
poi	edible purple paste made from taro root
pollo	chicken
pupusa	soft baked bread w/ shredded meat inside
sombrero	large Mexican hats
wahine	women
windward	situated on the side facing the wind

THE JOY WEAVER - GRASSROOTS

Notes

1. J. Roberto Moncado R, Ralph Lee Woodward, and Wayne M. Clegern. "Honduras." Britannica. Accessed December 1, 2021. https://www.britannica.com/place/Honduras .

2. J. Roberto Moncado R, Ralph Lee Woodward, and Wayne M. Clegern. "Honduras." Britannica. Accessed December 1, 2021. https://www.britannica.com/place/Honduras .

3. Kerri Lee Alexander. "Queen Liliuokalani." National Women's History Museum. 2020. https://www.womenshistory.org/education-resources/biographies/queen-liliuokalani .

4. "USS Arizona (BB-39)." Wikipedia. Accessed November 22, 2021. https://www.en.widipedia.org/wiki/USS_Arizona_(BB39) .

5. Jackson. "Stairway to Heaven Hike on Oahu, Hawaii: Updated 2021." Journey Era. May 17, 2021 https://www.journey-era.com/stairway-to-heaven-oahu-hawaii .

6. "Opana Radar Site." Wikipedia. Accessed January 7, 2023. https://www.en.wikipedia.org/wiki/Opana_Radar_Site

7. "Hawaii State Song: Hawai'I Pono'i." ERD ereferencedesk. Accessed December 4, 2021. https://www.ereferencedesk.com/resources/state-song/hawaii.html#:~:text=Origin%20of%20Song%3A%20%22Hawai%27i%20Pono%27i%22%20The%20Hawaiian%20Kingdom%27s,Monarch%22%2C%20founder%20of%20the%20Hawaiian%20Kingdom%20in%201810 .

8. "Sunday Program Inaugurates New F.M. Radio Service." Star Bulletin. November 3, 1953. Clipped by sammibri. Newspaper.com. Clipped by sammibri. https://www.newspapers.com/clip/30620637/sunday-program-inaugurates-new-fm

9. "Construction Permit and License Record." getimportletter_exh.cgi. KAIM-FM. Slides #5/19 and #16/19. Accessed November 24, 2021. https://www.licensing.fcc.gov/cgibin/prod/cdbs/forms/prod/getimportletter_exh.cgi?import_letter_id=71019.

10. "Types of Butterfly > Butterflies in USA > Butterfly Facts." Butterfly Identification. Accessed December 13, 2021. https://www.butterflyidentification.com/painted-lady.htm and https://wwwbutterflyidentification.com/kamehameha-butterfly.htm .

11. NOAA Hawaiian Islands Humpback Whale National Marine Sanctuary. "Grade 3 Unit 5 Why Humpback Whales Migrate from Alaska to Hawaii." Coast.noaa.gov. Accessed November 30, 2021. Slides #5-7, 16, 19, 21, 28.
https://coast.noaa.gov/data/SEAMedia/Presenttions/PDFs/Grade%203%20Unit%205%20Lesson%203%20Why%20Huback%20Whales%20Migrate%20from%20Alaska%20to%20Hawaii.pdf#:~:text=Migration%20is%20usually%20a%20response%20to%20changes%20in,grounds%20in%20the%20warmer%20waters%20of%20tropical%20regions

12. NOAA Hawaiian Islands Humpback Whale National Marine Sanctuary. "Grade 4 Unit 4 Humpback Whales – The Basics." Coast.noaa.gov. Accessed November 30, 2021. Slides #20-22, 46-52. https://coast.noaa.gov/data/SEAMedia/Presentations/PDFs/Grade%204%20Unit%204%20Lesson%202%20Humpback%20Whale%20Basics.pdf#:~:text=Humpback%20Whale%20Identification%2040%20%E2%80%93%2050%20feet%20long%21,adults%20can%20weigh%2040-50%20tons.%20That%E2%80%99s%2080%2C000-90%2C000%20pounds%21

13. David Keirsey, Marilyn Bates, *Please Understand Me: Character & Temperament Types*, (Del Mar, CA: Gnosology Books Ltd, 1984).

14. D. James Kennedy, PH.D., *The Real Meaning of the Zodiac*, (Albert Lea, MN: D. James Kennedy Ministries, 1989), 19-20.

15. Fitts, Bob, *One God*, Hosanna! Music, 1993, accessed 9-30-22, https://www.youtube.com/watch?v=Y6DlmJ-s9WU

16. Dr. John Booth, *Equipping for Effective Marriage* (Phoenix, AZ: Paradise Valley Counseling Inc., 1990).

17. Caswall, Edwards, *When Morning Gilds the Skies, Favorite Hymns of Praise*, (Wheaton, IL: Tabernacle Publishing Company, 1967), 1.

18. Gaither Vocal Band, *Beyond the Open Door*, Track #7, A Few Good Men, Star Song Communications, 1992, CD. Lyrics written by Shawn Craig.

Made in the USA
Middletown, DE
18 March 2023

27010475R00130